Images of Modern America

CRUISING IN MONTGOMERY AND BERKS COUNTIES

On the Front Cover: New Hanover United Methodist Church on Swamp Pike in Gilbertsville, Pennsylvania, held their annual Car & Bike Show on September 15, 2014. The show featured music, food, awards, and prizes, and the event benefitted Happy 2 Be Home. (Courtesy of New Hanover Methodist Church.)

On the Upper Back Cover: Grandview Speedway in the 1980s (courtesy of Charles Grebe Jr.)

On the Lower Back Cover: (from left to right) Good Old Days of Pottstown! Then and Now Cruise and Car Show 2015 (courtesy of George Zlumlord Watters), Mark Rubright racing at Maple Grove Raceway (courtesy of Mark Rubright), North End Cruise In in Pottstown, Pennsylvania (courtesy of Mark Rubright)

Images of Modern America

CRUISING IN MONTGOMERY AND BERKS COUNTIES

Tina M. Kissinger

ARCADIA PUBLISHING

ISBN 978-1-4671-1557-5

Published by Arcadia Publishing
Charleston, South Carolina

Printed in the United States of America

Library of Congress Control Number: 2015948513

For all general information, please contact Arcadia Publishing:
Telephone 843-853-2070
Fax 843-853-0044
E-mail sales@arcadiapublishing.com
For customer service and orders:
Toll-Free 1-888-313-2665

Visit us on the Internet at www.arcadiapublishing.com

I would like to dedicate this book to the cruisers, race car drivers, and people who make wonderful car shows happen in Montgomery and Berks Counties. No matter which generation we came from, it is in all of our hearts and minds. May we continue to cruise and show our love of fast cars, the sound of turning the corner at the track, and spending warm nights showing off our restored cars.

Contents

ACKNOWLEDGMENTS

This book was made possible because we are lucky enough to have several amateur and professional photographers in Montgomery and Berks Counties. I want to thank the many historians that contributed information and helped introduce me to those in the car community. They provided the history of our local tracks and their own personal stories, memories, and love of cars.

I would like to thank my editor at Arcadia Publishing, Caitrin Cunningham, for her advice and encouragement. Thanks also go to several local car enthusiasts; specifically, I would like to thank Joe Jordan, Doug Mentzer, Mark Rubright, Brad Ray, Tony Ziemba, Paul Ziemba, Rick Huff, Ron and Matt Peck, George Zlumlord Watters, Fred Spiezio, Steve D. Sabo, Michael Shaub, Scott Hartman, Bill Kissinger, Bill Salter, Carl Rubrecht, John Puccella, Eric Swarr, Thomas McGinn, and many more.

Finally, thanks goes to my loving family and friends who have always been there to support me in this and all endeavors. Thank you to my boyfriend, Robert Bright, for the encouragement during long nights of research and writing.

INTRODUCTION

Car enthusiasts live and play throughout Montgomery and Berks Counties in Pennsylvania. Cars have always been important to the people in this area. When looking for something to do, especially on the weekends, car enthusiasts have come to the right place. There are always great car events happening in both counties.

Amazing car shows are held in this region from spring to fall, and many eagerly await the end of winter in anticipation of new adventures. The planning of shows often starts months in advance by a knowledgeable and excited group of people. They reach out to those who love to restore cars and present them to the public. It takes hard work, but it is worth it when an event is held. Hundreds come out to show their appreciation of cars and trucks of the past and present.

Some enthusiasts enjoy a specific make or model—and the year is often important, too. Others come to car shows in hopes of finding a car they used to own or something they may be saving money for in the future. The shows offer a chance to get outside, to meet old friends, to reminisce about the good old days, and to meet new people. Events are even held on holidays such as Father's Day, Fourth of July, and Labor Day. Car clubs drive their cars in parades, often with the mayor or homecoming queen as a special guest. Most car shows will sponsor a family or child in need. People in the communities are helpful and often raise a lot of money for a good cause, which makes the shows even nicer to attend. Trophies and plaques are given for many categories, and it is a real honor to receive either. The enthusiasm is always visible at the shows across Montgomery and Berks Counties.

Did you or your friends cruise on a regular basis—or even for just one night? It may have been in a town such as Pottstown, Hatboro, or Lansdale in Montgomery County. These towns have become known as far away as the West Coast for fast cars and street racing, which made for a fantastic cruising experience. The cruising years represented a great time in many people's lives—a time they have never forgotten, filled with driving down favorite streets, hanging out with friends, and enjoying the music streaming out of car windows as laughter filled the cars and parking lots and everyone enjoyed the fun.

Many could not wait for the weekend—or even the end of the week—to start cruising. Hundreds, even thousands, of people filled the streets to spend a few hours talking about cars and watching the streets get brighter with every new car that found its way to the pavement. American flags could be seen flying in the back of trucks as drivers showed their patriotic sides. Waiting at the next traffic light was a chance to meet new friends or just to wave hello. For the cruisers, it was impossible not to enjoy themselves.

Cruising changed over the years due to restrictions that many were not happy about. Even with these restrictions, the good times are still remembered. We will not forget the memories, which is why reunion cruises are still held throughout the spring and summer months. Many enjoy taking photographs to remember the past and to show future generations. During cruises, people gather on the sidewalks as they wave at and pick out their favorite cars. The participants really enjoy the chance to reminisce and to have a chance to bring cruising back to these great towns. Some towns have "Cruise Ins" after car-show events, and people gather around a restaurant or in a parking lot to relax during the warm nights, just like old times. Flyers and posts are shared on the Internet to help people find out when a cruise will be held, and old-fashioned word of mouth travels fast before a local cruise, as plenty of cruisers are ready to have fun.

The stories of these cruisers have been told in several ways, including in national car magazines such as *Hot Rod* and *Car Craft* during the 1980s. These days, videos of famous cruising places such as Pottstown, Pennsylvania, can be found on YouTube. We were lucky enough to have a videographer and cruiser—George Zlumlord Watters—who filmed while watching cruisers on High Street in Pottstown. Today, cruisers are celebrated in blogs and articles found online, and with each new form of media, Montgomery and Berks Counties have been well represented. Countless former cruisers decided to make a living working on cars in both counties. Auto shops fill the area due to these cruisers' expertise and history of driving and working on cars. Even large companies in the area—such as Dana Corporation, Firestone, and Neapco—hired local men and women to build cars and car parts in their facilities. Generation after generation has learned this trade, making Montgomery and Berks Counties not only a place for fun but also for hard work.

Racing has brought national attention to Berks and Montgomery Counties. Well-known tracks such as Mill Park and Sanatoga Speedway—both located in Pottstown—attracted stock car racers including brothers Moose and Harry Moore, Red Lesher, Bobby Ryan, and many more. In Pennsylvania, drivers could also be found at tracks like Dorney Park Speedway in Allentown, Vargo Dragstrip in Perkasie, Hatfield Speedway in Hatfield, Reading Fairgrounds Speedway in Reading, Grandview Speedway in Bechtsville, and Maple Grove Raceway in Mohnton. Over the years, some have closed, but memories of the smell of oil, the cheering crowds, and winners' names being called over the loudspeaker remain fresh in people's minds. Some tracks have stayed open and flourished, luring huge crowds of fans who eagerly wait for the gates to open on race days. They fill the grandstands in search of new champions, great food, and the chance to meet old and new friends. Families have followed each other to the track for decades while enjoying the sport of racing and a chance to spend time together. The races have a special place in the hearts of all who enjoy cruising, no matter their age.

Together, we will continue to make memories, be hard workers, and have fun at any car event we choose to attend in Montgomery and Berks Counties.

One

Cruising

Hot Summer Nights

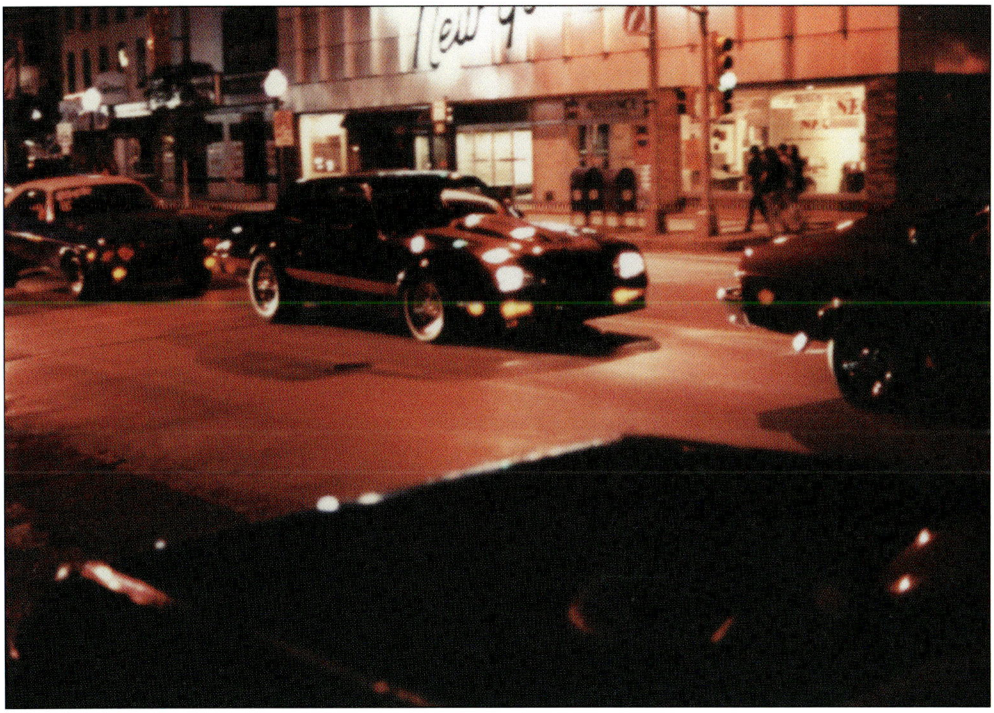

The cars light up on High Street in Pottstown, Pennsylvania, in the early 1990s, as they drive up from East High Street. Cruising usually started in the early evening and ended around 2:00 a.m., with some people cruising around Dempsey's Diner until 4:00 a.m. A popular hangout was the Coventry Mall, where cruisers would play in the arcades (Games People Play and the Gold Mine) before meeting on High Street. Zerns Farmers Market was another place frequented by cruisers, who walked around and played games in the arcade. (Courtesy of John Puccella.)

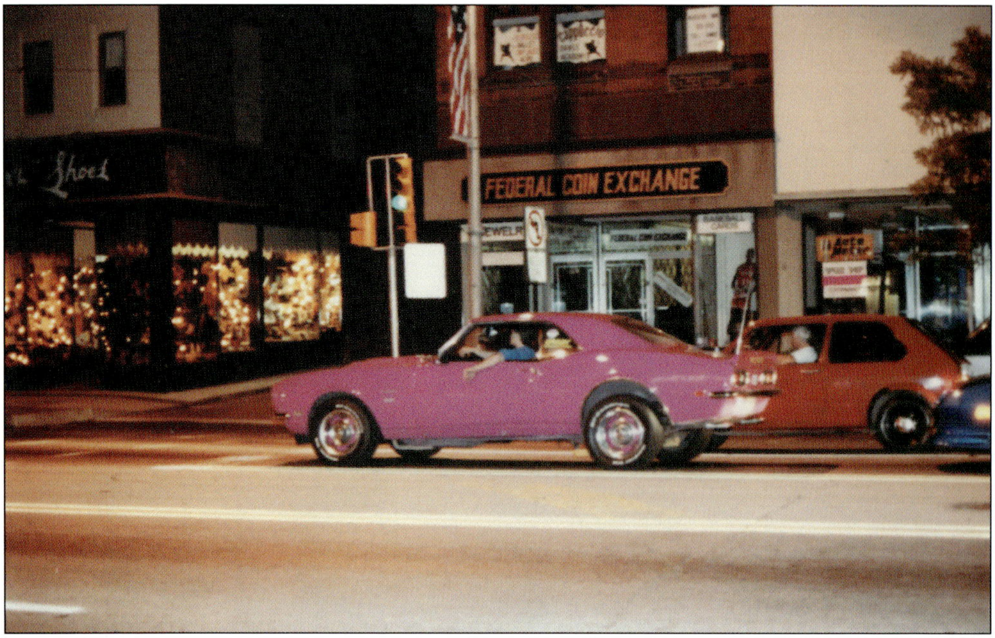

Cars cruise up High Street near Penn Street on a late 1990s night. Federal Coin Exchange, Woolworth, and Newberry Company are stores that were popular in Pottstown at the time. People enjoyed saying hello to friends as they showed off their cars. Many cruisers would meet at Dempsey's Diner to turn around, while others headed down to 7-Eleven in the east end of Pottstown. Each night, friends would contact each other to see where they planned to meet, and sometimes they would say, "I'll meet you Outtown," so they could talk to each other and relax. Cruisers' favorite hangouts were the Security National Bank, the corner of High and Hanover Streets, a parking lot at Evans and High Streets, Pep Boys, on the wall at the PNC Bank, and the Hill school across from Midtown Tire. Many listened to their favorite songs on the radio. The CB radio was also very popular to use while cruising, as cellphones were not yet accessible to mainstream consumers. (Both, courtesy of John Puccella.)

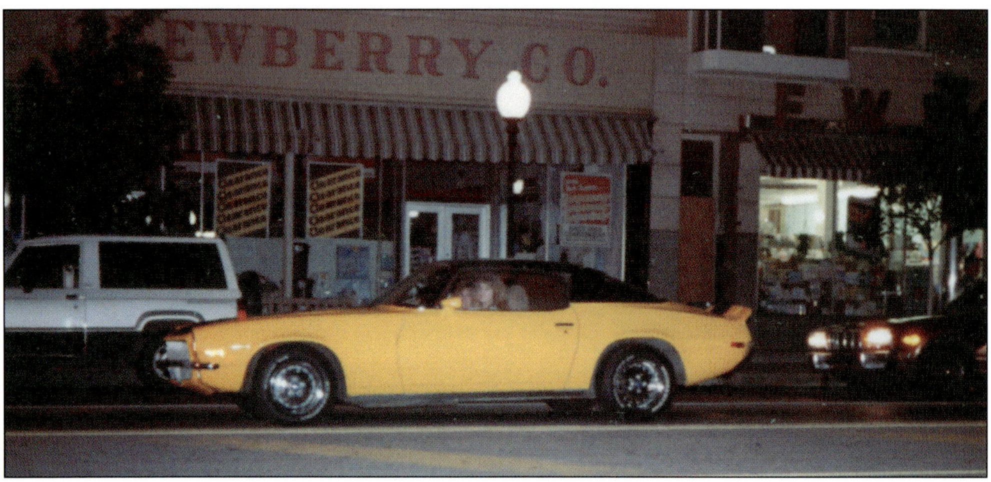

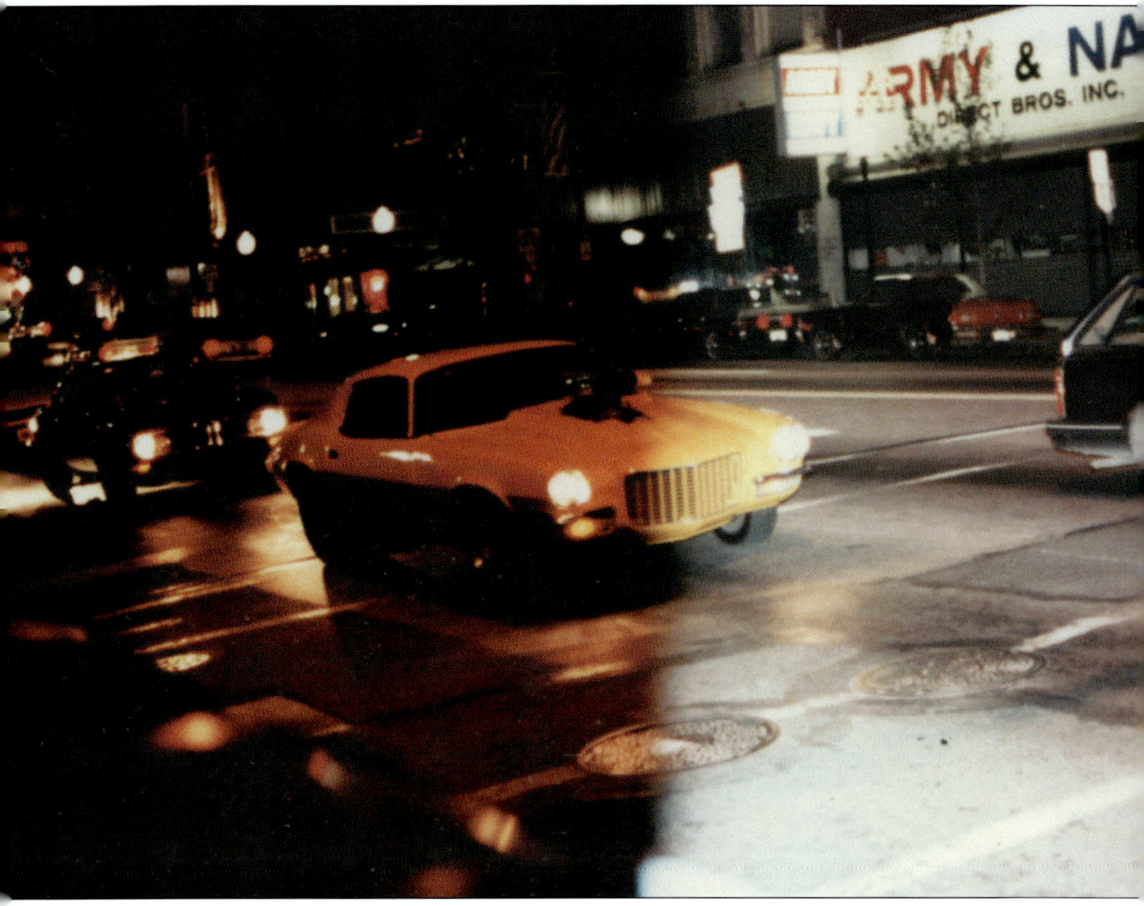

Jeff Fern, or "Pro Jeff," of Pennsburg, cruised High Street in Pottstown starting in 1981 with his Pro/Street 1970s Camaro. He really enjoyed cruising and working on his car, making this car great throughout the years. Pro Jeff can often be found at car shows and Cruise Ins and is happy to talk about his car's transformation since his early days of cruising. (Courtesy of John Puccella.)

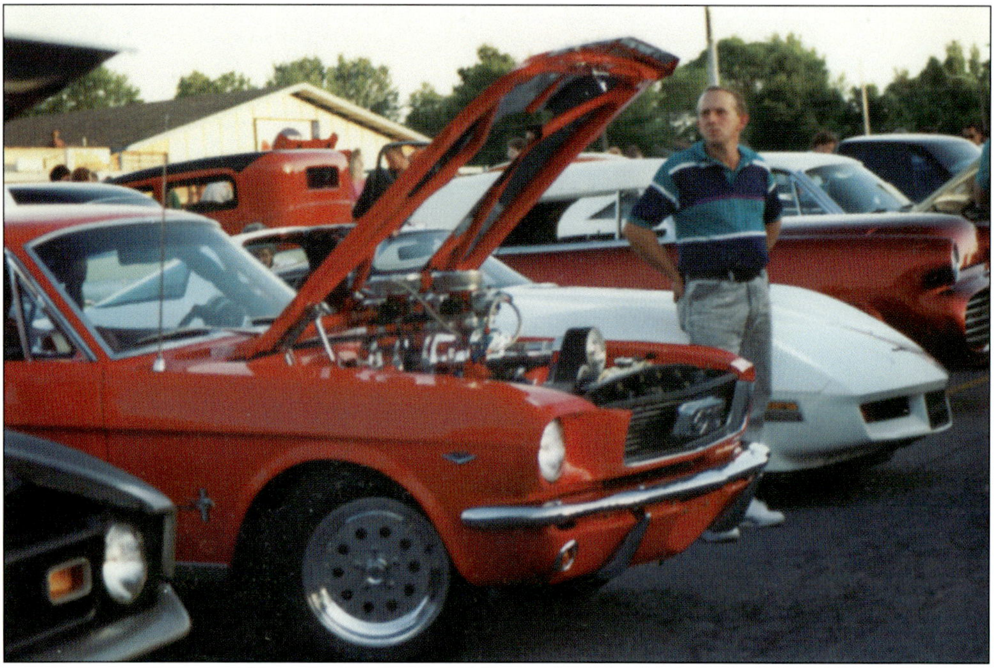

Ray Mayer, owner of Performance Specialties, exhibits his Speed Shop Mustang during the North End Shopping Center Cruise In in 1988. Mayer's shop is located at 323 High Street in Pottstown. Mayer has been involved with promoting cruising for years, organizing and holding car shows at his business, and continues racing. (Courtesy of Mark Rubright.)

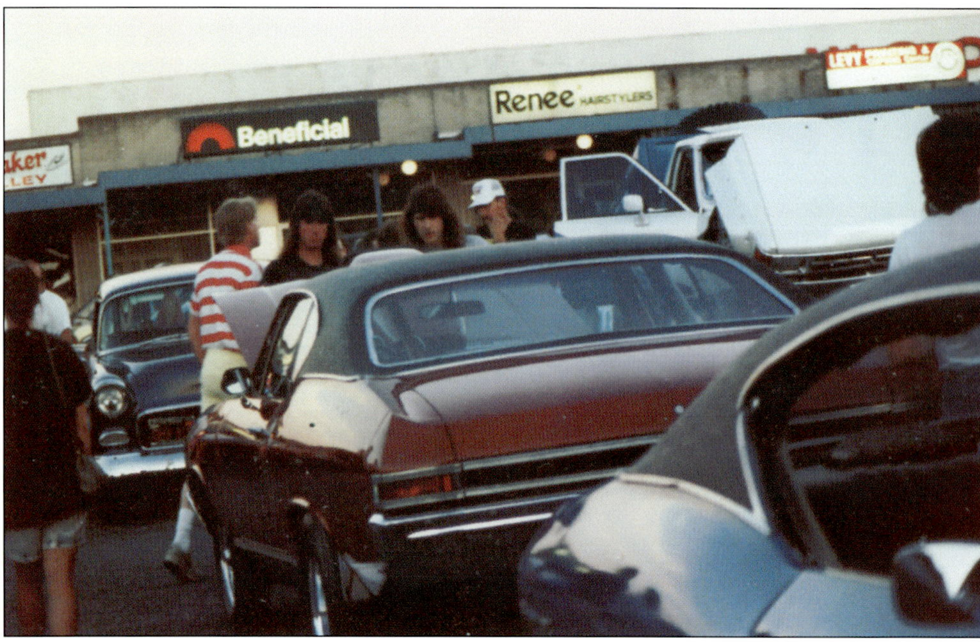

The late Todd Detweiler (left) and Mark Rubright look at Rubright's 1968 Chevrolet Chevelle at the North End Shopping Center Cruise In in Pottstown. The event gave them a chance to show their cars before heading out to cruise on High Street in Pottstown. Friendships made through cruising have lasted a lifetime. (Courtesy of Mark Rubright.)

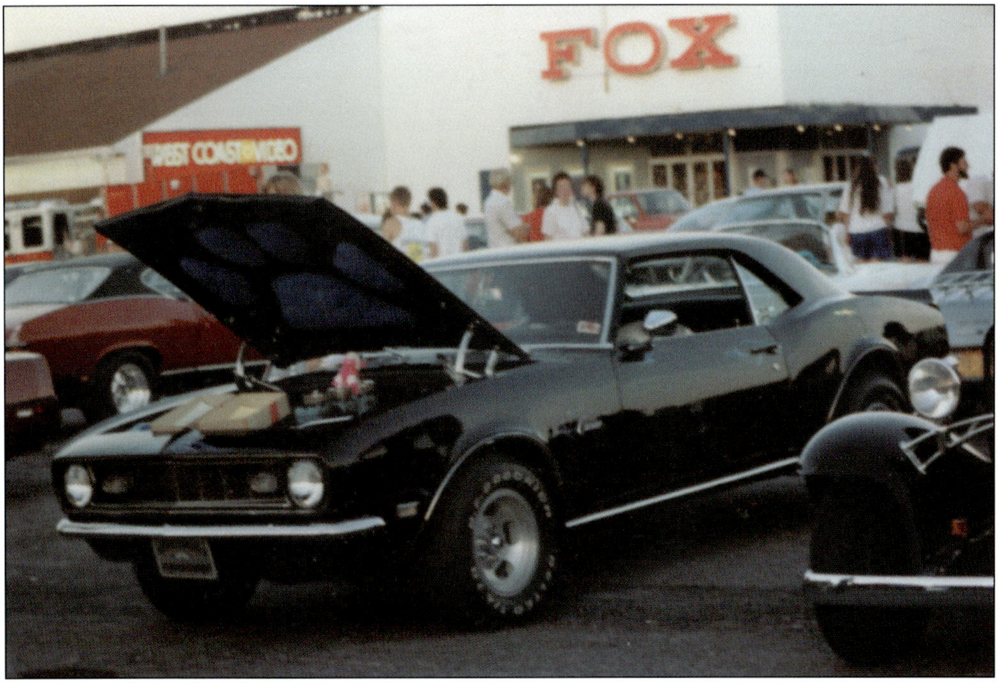

A black 1969 Chevy Camaro is on display at the North End Shopping Center Cruise In, sponsored by East End Car Club, in 1988. West Coast Video and the Fox Theatre are visible in the background. People would drive to Pottstown from surrounding areas—and even from California—since it was such a well-known place to see the hottest cars. (Courtesy of Mark Rubright.)

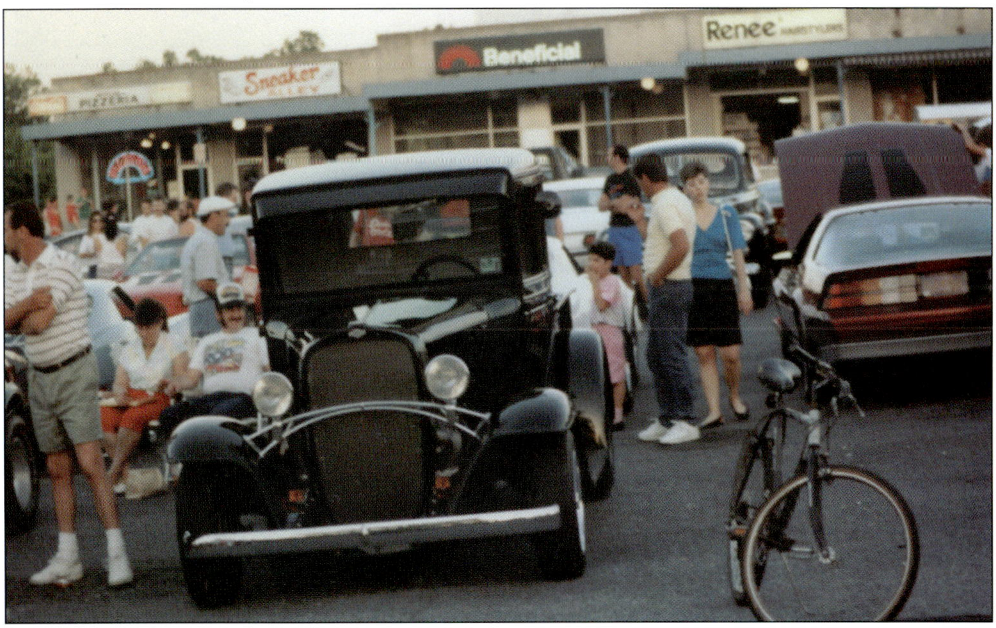

A 1930s Chevy pickup truck is pictured at the North End Shopping Center Cruise In in 1988. Everyone, including children, came out to see the unique cars and trucks. The shopping center was a nice place for the cruise in, as there were many different stores and restaurants in the area. A hobby shop also stood on the property, which many visited. (Courtesy of Mark Rubright.)

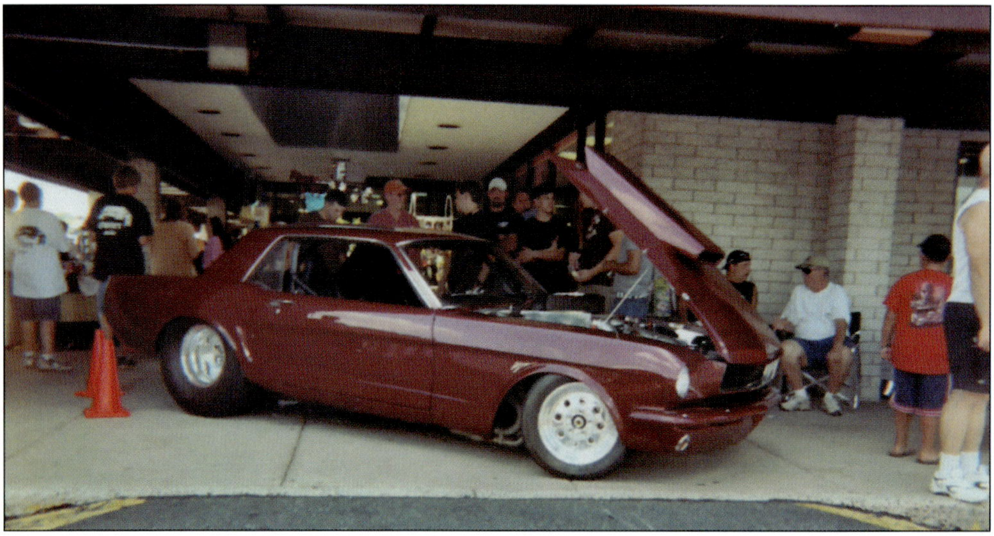

Jim Swarr's 1965 Mustang, a big-block Chevy powered with nitrous oxide, is pictured here on display at a car show. The Mustang had a stick shift and was street-driven on pump gas. Swarr was well known for many things, including cruising. As a cruiser, he was involved with the Pottstown Cruising Association, which supported other cruisers on High Street in Pottstown. He would often help them fight for their right to cruise. Swarr was a car enthusiast who was very secretive about his car and made sure he always was the only one under his hood. Known as "King of the Streets," he was a street car driver who would race anyone in Pottstown as well as other towns. (Courtesy of Mark Rubright.)

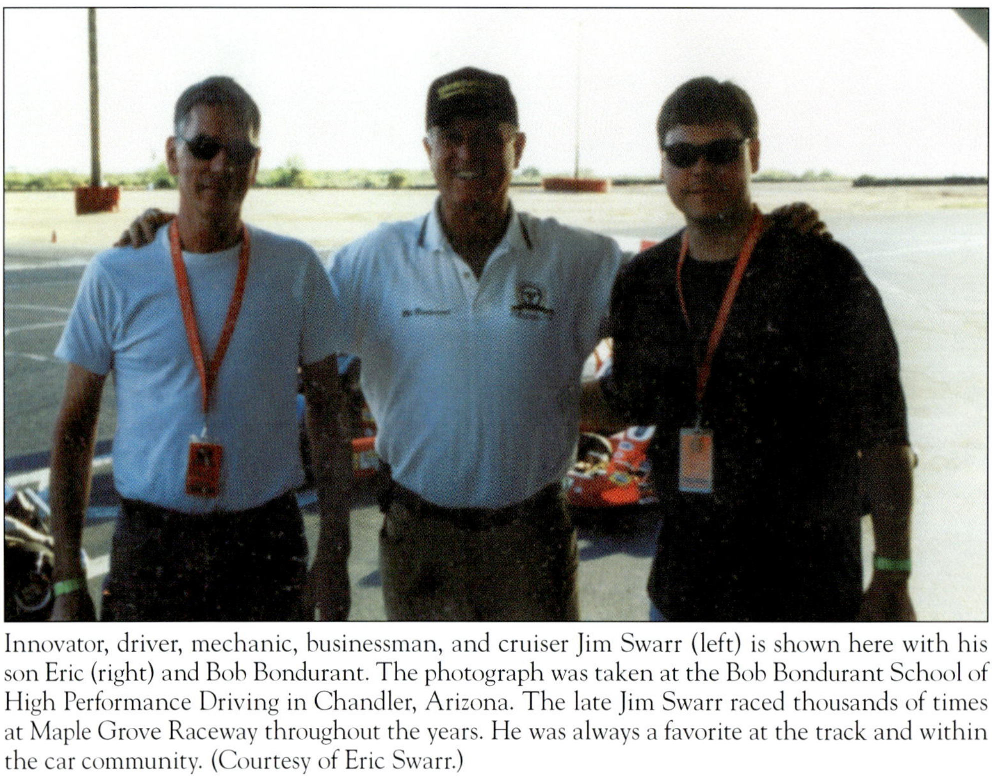

Innovator, driver, mechanic, businessman, and cruiser Jim Swarr (left) is shown here with his son Eric (right) and Bob Bondurant. The photograph was taken at the Bob Bondurant School of High Performance Driving in Chandler, Arizona. The late Jim Swarr raced thousands of times at Maple Grove Raceway throughout the years. He was always a favorite at the track and within the car community. (Courtesy of Eric Swarr.)

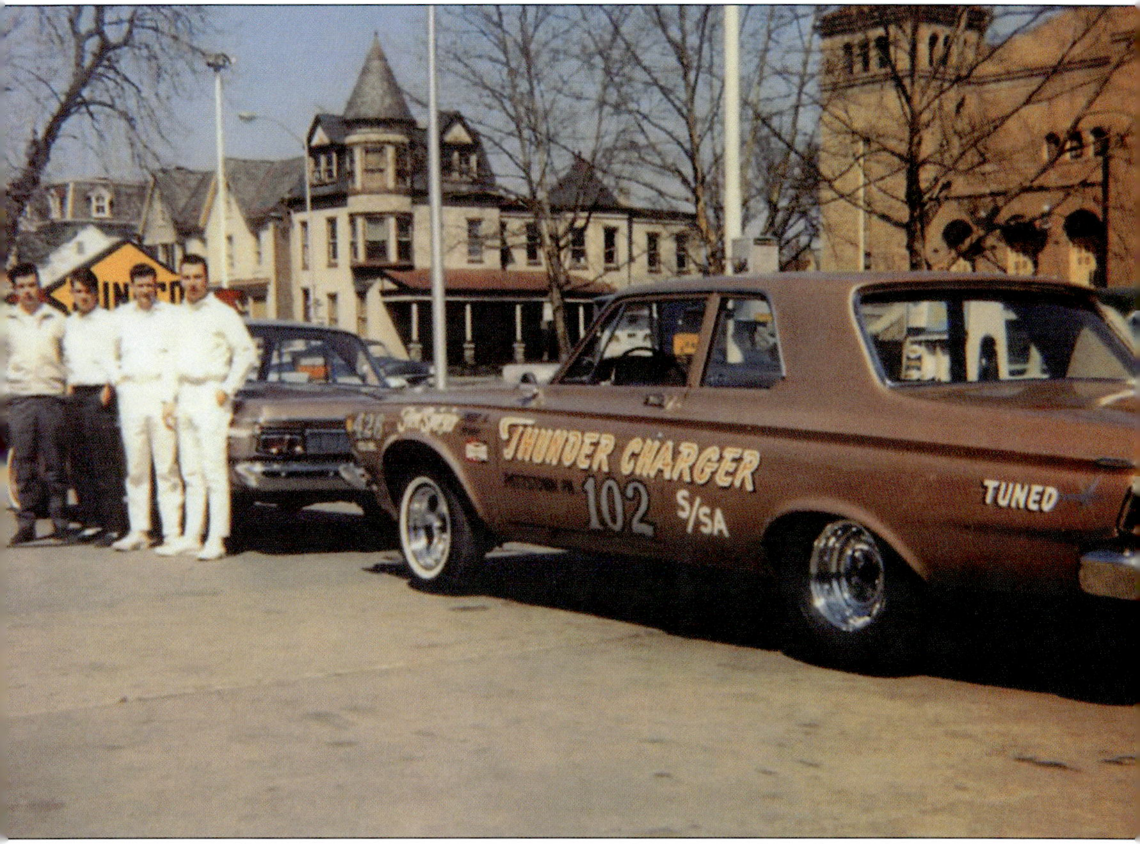

Fred Spiezio started cruising in Pottstown in 1948. He took a lot of pride in driving his 1956 Dodge 501 Thunder Charger on High Street, which he did for many years. Spiezio took this photograph of a crew at Bart's Sunoco, located at the corner of High and Adams Streets, in the 1960s. Spiezio always attends local car shows in the area. (Courtesy of Fred Spiezio.)

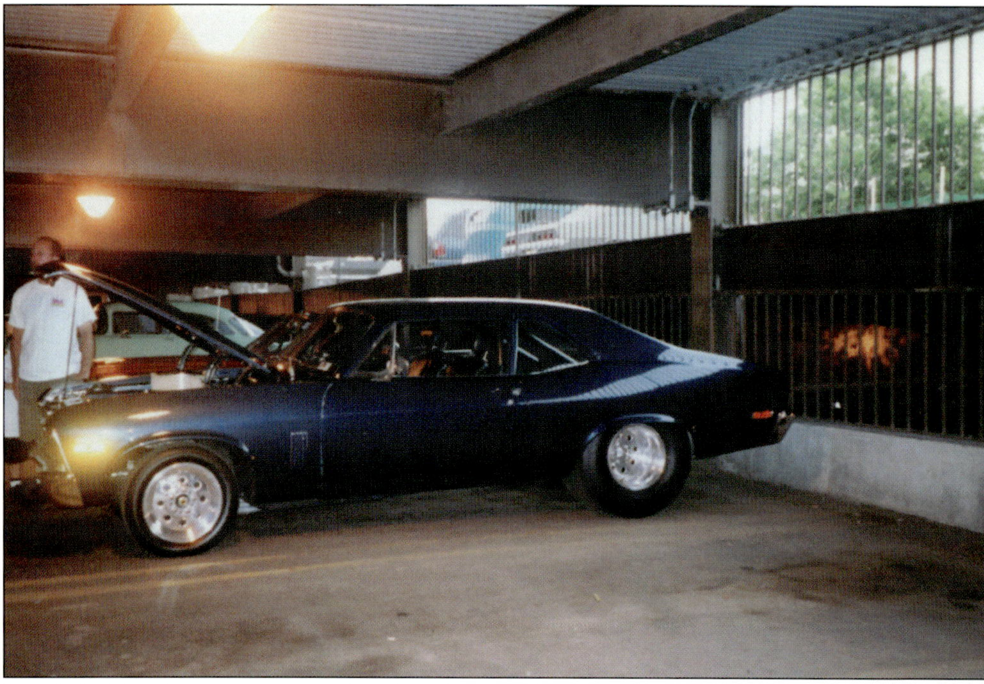

Randy Robbins's Nova is pictured at New England Nationals in Worcester, Massachusetts, in 1997. Robbins was very involved in cruising on High Street in Pottstown from 1982 until the cruising ended in the middle of 2000. He had a big block Chevy in it, which helped him to not only cruise but also to street race on US Route 422. (Courtesy of Mark Rubright.)

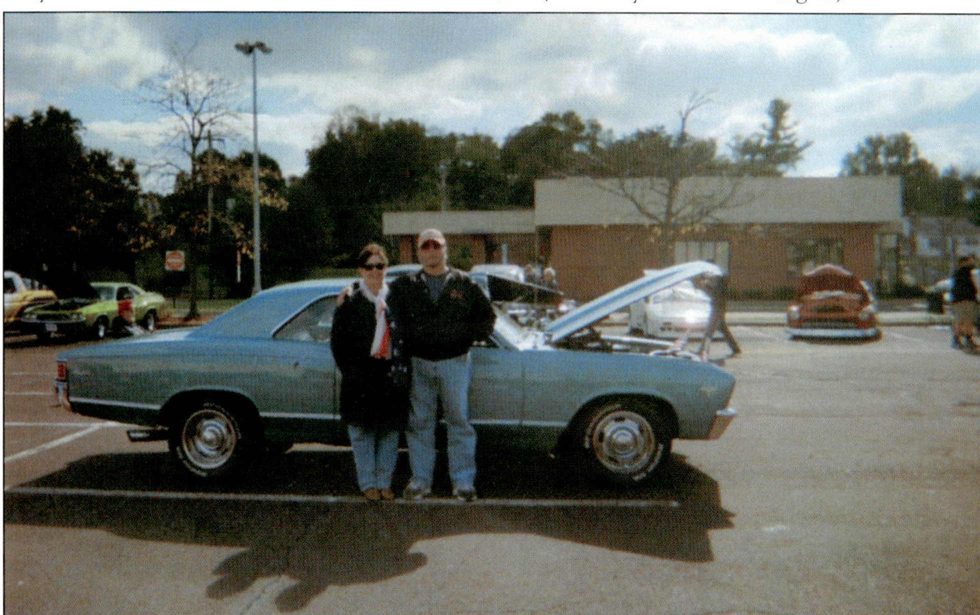

Terry and Angie Hallman are pictured here on October 5, 2014, at the third annual North Coventry Police Department's Fallen Hero Auto Show at Coventry Mall. They met cruising on High Street in Pottstown. Their car is a 1967 Chevelle Malibu big block, which they have owned for 11 years. (Courtesy of Alvin Clark.)

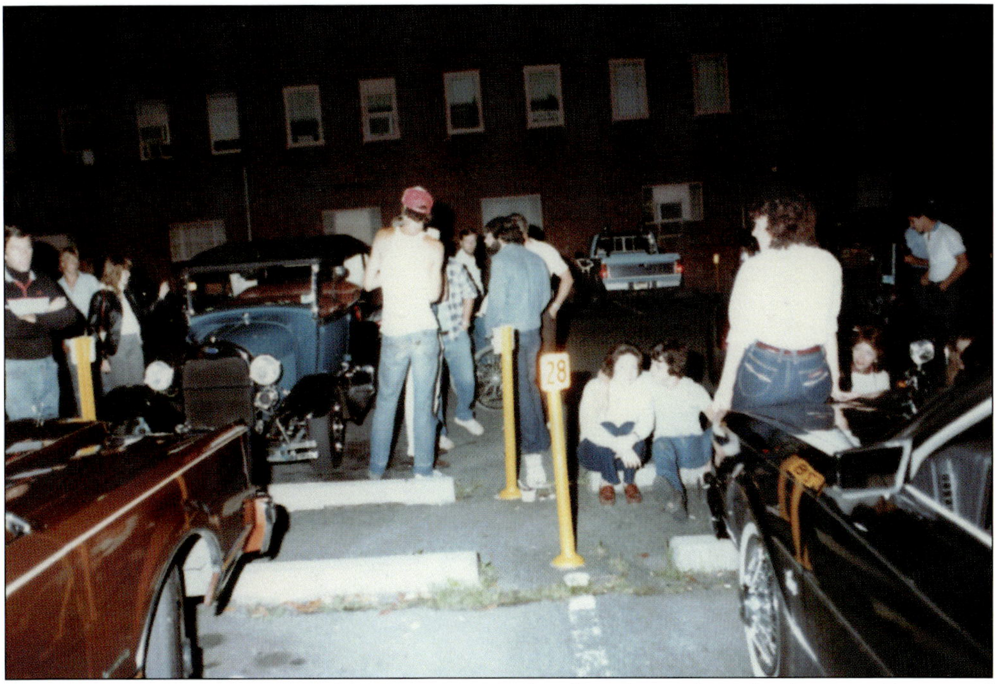

In the mid-1980s, cruisers would meet every weekend in the parking lot between Evans and Franklin Streets to hang out and talk about their cars. Schoolmates, drivers, and mechanics all had a place to enjoy seeing everyone each weekend. The cruising scene in Pottstown was featured in national magazines such as *Hot Rod*. The meet-up became well known for all types of vehicles, which represented the area. Everyone would leave at some point during the evening to cruise up to the end of town. Many enjoyed sitting on their cars, listening to music, and taking pictures. A normal night included cruising up and down High Street several times before returning to the parking lot. The money spent for gas used in a personal car was not an issue; they cruised for fun and, often, bragging rights. (Courtesy of Fred Spiezio.)

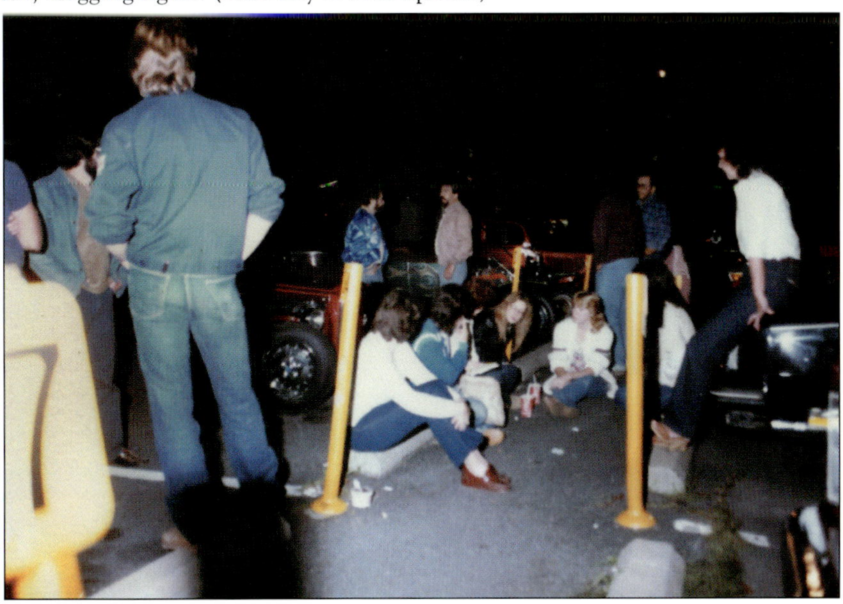

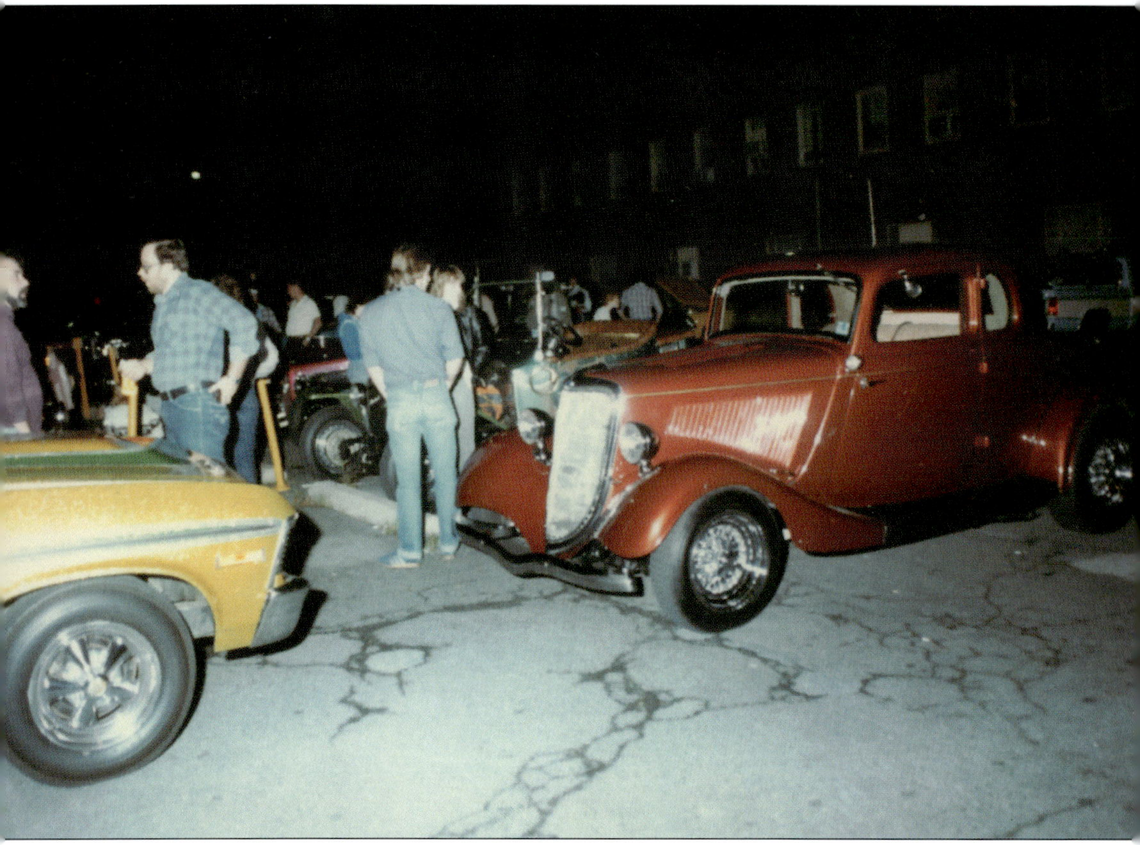

Cruisers brought car trailers into Pottstown from all over the country. Drivers cruised on High Street to show how fast and loud their cars could be. Plenty of cars raced on the bypass and in neighboring cities. Each night brought new experiences and faster cars. (Courtesy of Fred Spiezio.)

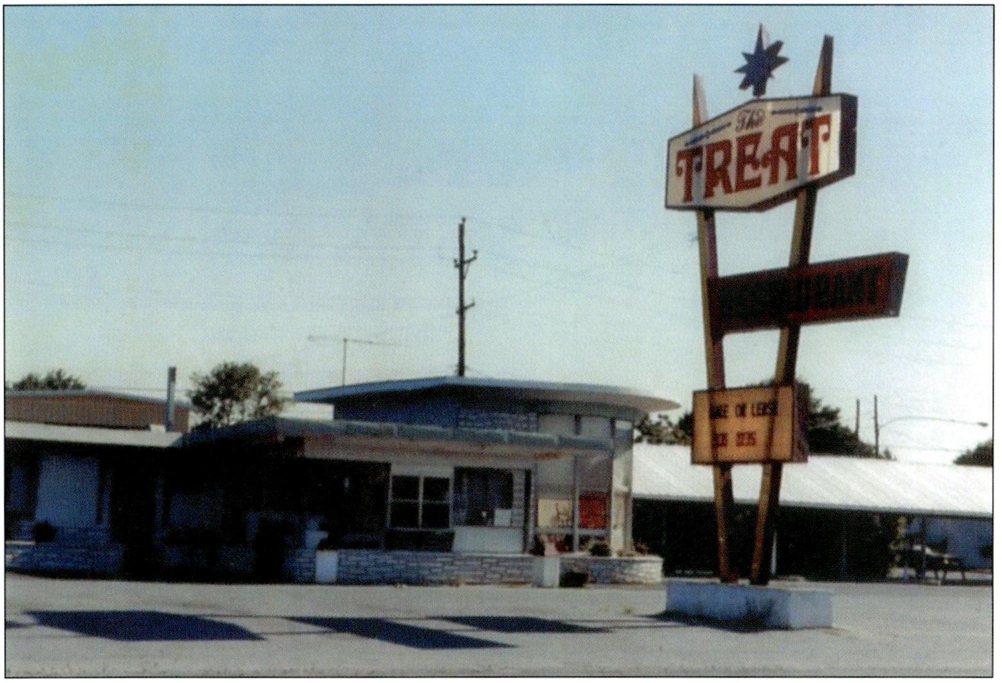

Phillips Drive In, also known as the Tropical Treat, opened in Stowe, Pennsylvania, in 1955. It became a very popular restaurant for the cruising population in Pottstown. Many would drive from the east end of Pottstown to "the Treat" to enjoy their wonderful hamburgers, fries, milkshakes, and soft-serve ice cream. The cruisers continued to hang out at the Treat throughout the years. They often held car shows there, even after it closed. (Courtesy of Fred Spiezio.)

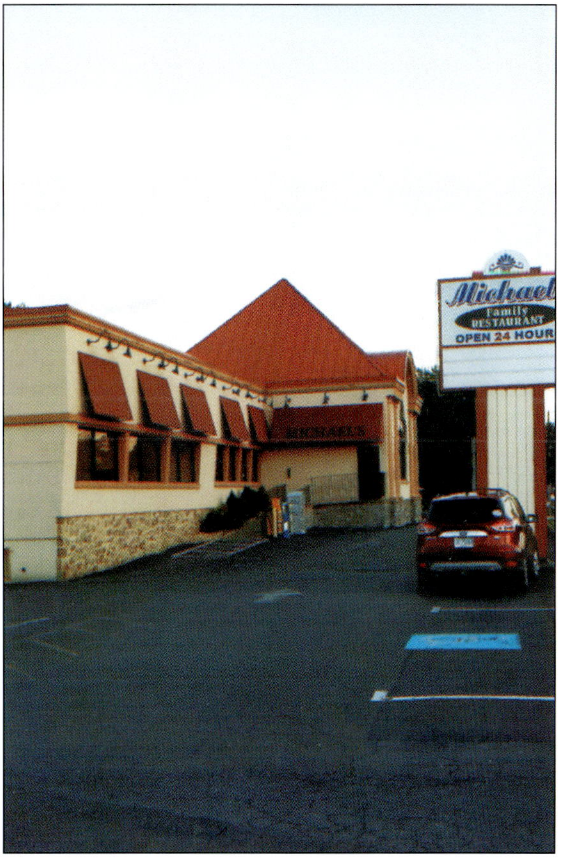

Michael's Restaurant has always been a popular place in Douglassville, Pennsylvania. Cruisers like to go there to eat and socialize after a long night of cruising High Street. It is open 24 hours a day and located in Berks County, which makes it easy to get to. Many cruisers enjoyed Michael's late-night breakfast, tasty desserts, and coffee, sometimes adding a little Tabasco sauce for a special treat. Michael's is a nice place to meet friends after hours. (Courtesy of Alvin Clark.)

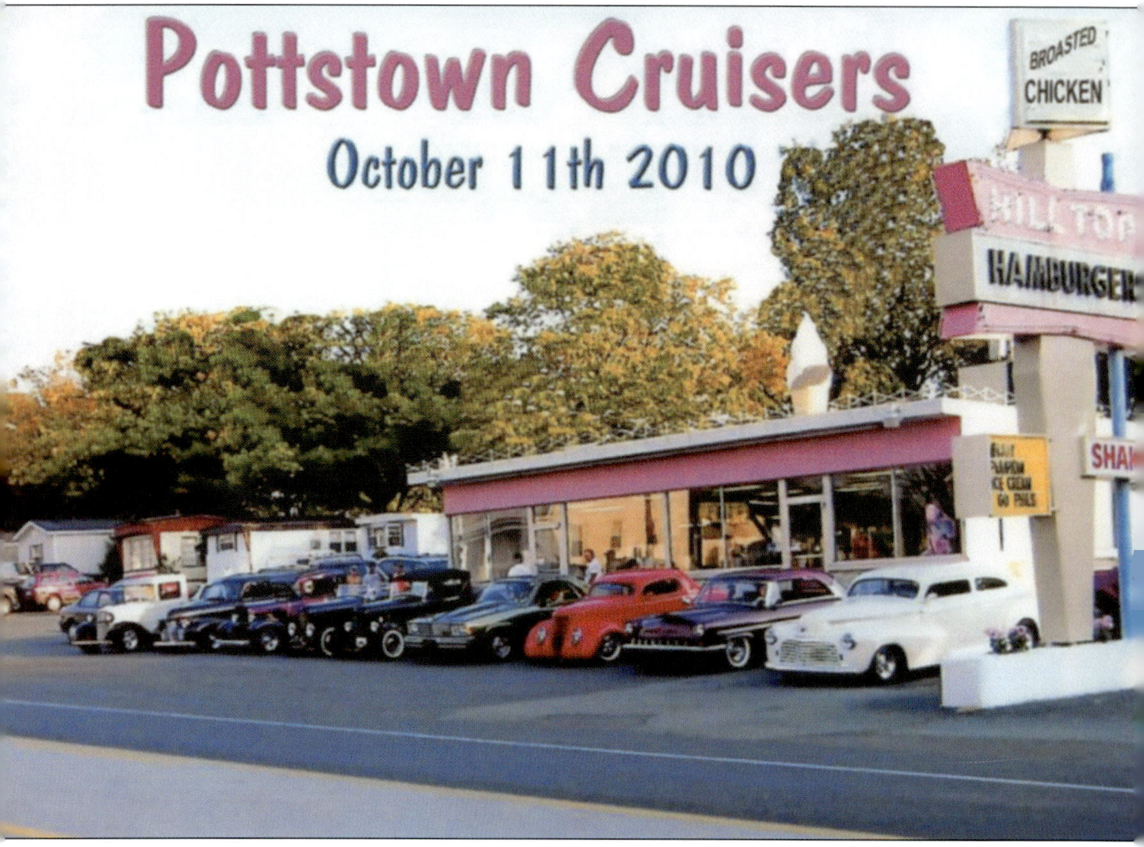

Pottstown Classics Car Club met at the Hilltop Drive-In, located in Pottstown, on October 11, 2010. Pottstown Classics Car Club welcomes all car enthusiasts—with or without a car. Their stated mission is: "Serving the Community through Our Hobby." This club helps the community with wonderful charitable events and car shows. (Courtesy of Fred Spiezio.)

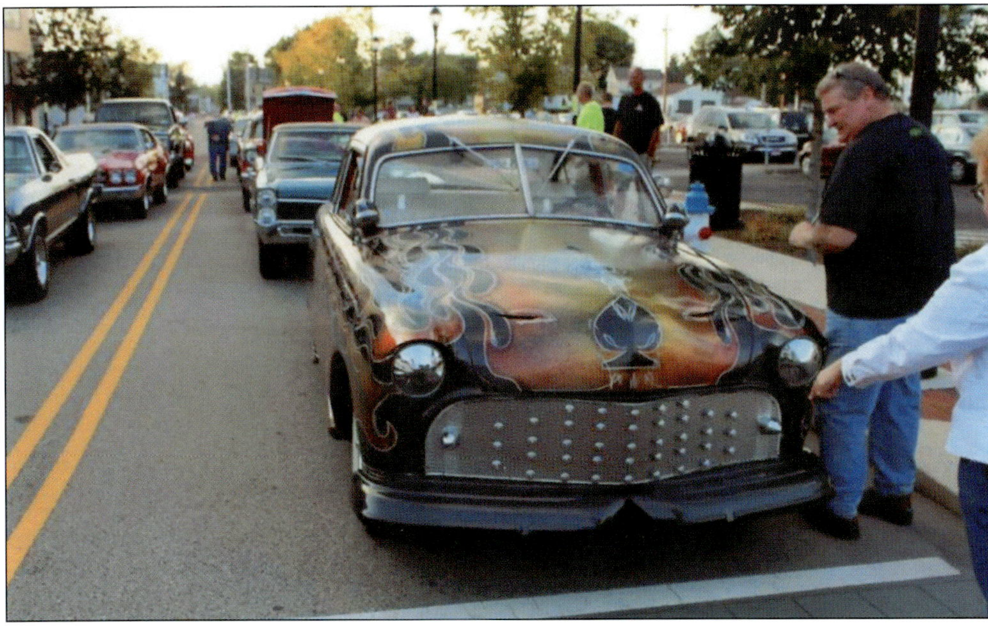

Lansdale cruisers enjoyed a night of remising and cruising in September 2014 during their annual cruise night. The annual cruise night was originally established as the Lansdale reunion cruise in a Facebook group called "I went cruzin' in Lansdale, PA and I'm Proud of it!" The group, which has over 1,604 members and is still growing, encourages members to help keep cruising alive. Each member has a chance to share memories and post pictures of new and past events. (Courtesy of Bill Salter.)

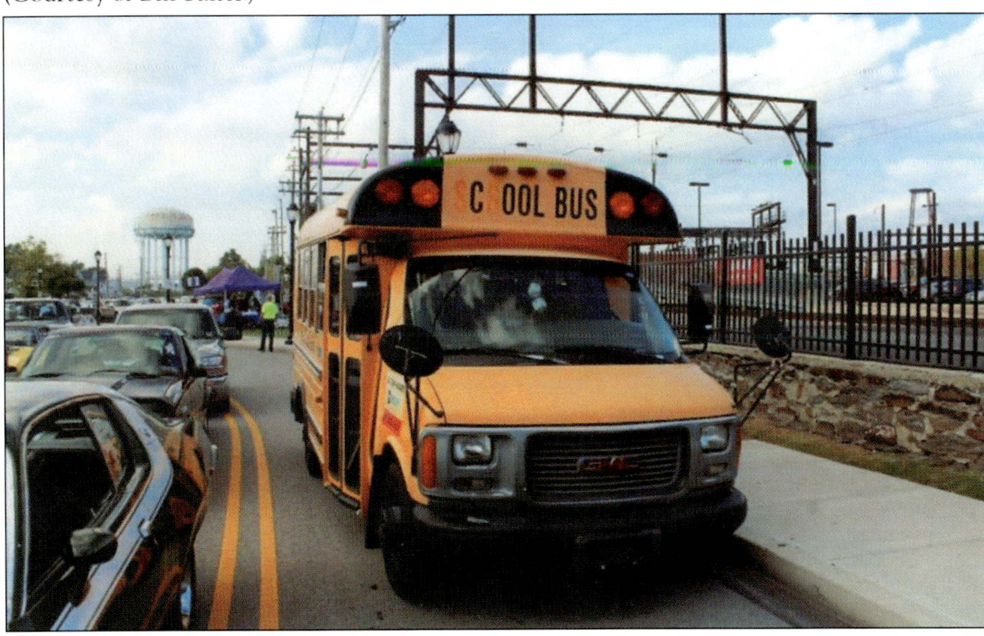

The "Cool Bus" makes it easy to cruise around Lansdale if one does not have a car during the annual reunion cruise. It is a modified school bus that people enjoy while taking in the sights of Lansdale. Anyone can ride the Cool Bus by offering a $2 donation to Manna, a nonprofit food pantry. (Courtesy of Bill Salter.)

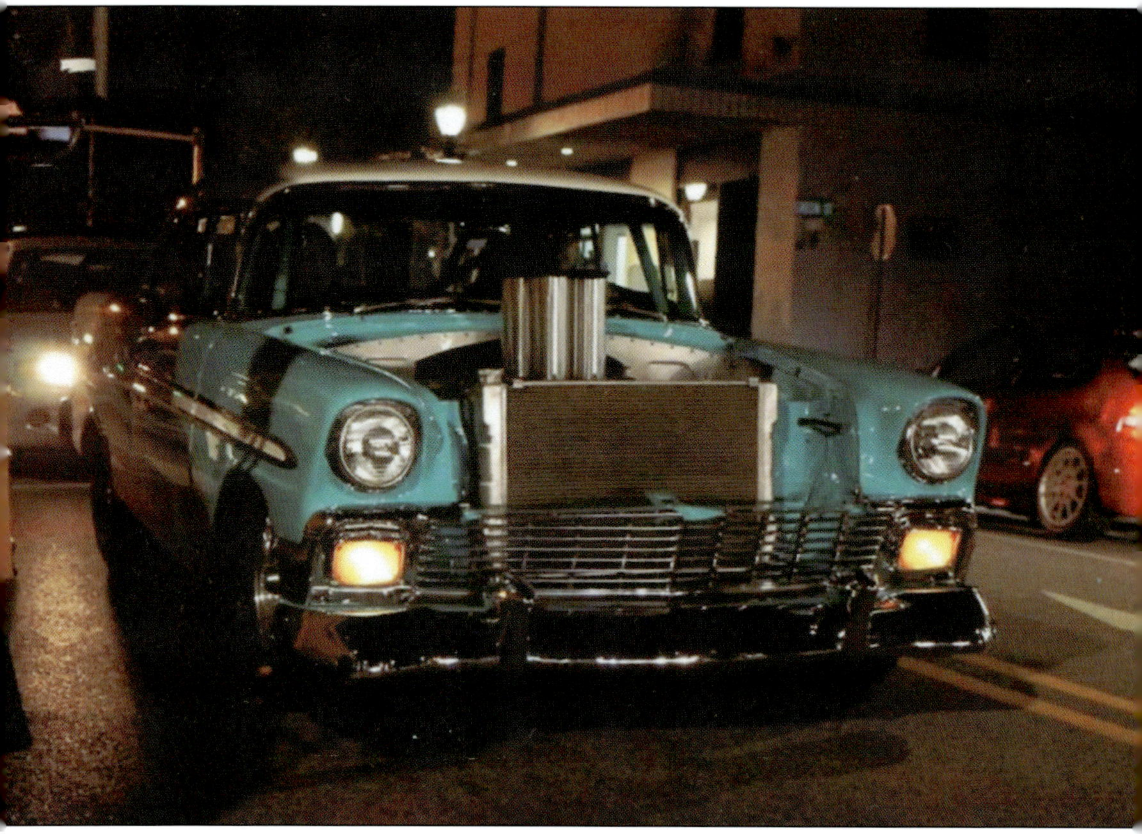

During a Lansdale reunion cruise, cruisers follow the same streets they once did, including West Main Street near Frank's Pizza, which used to be Nino's Pizza, where cruisers hung out in the restaurant's parking lot. They also still enjoy Nick's Pizza, which is still located in Lansdale. Cruisers would then drive to the I Got it at Gary's Plaza and the A&P grocery store. (Courtesy of Bill Salter.)

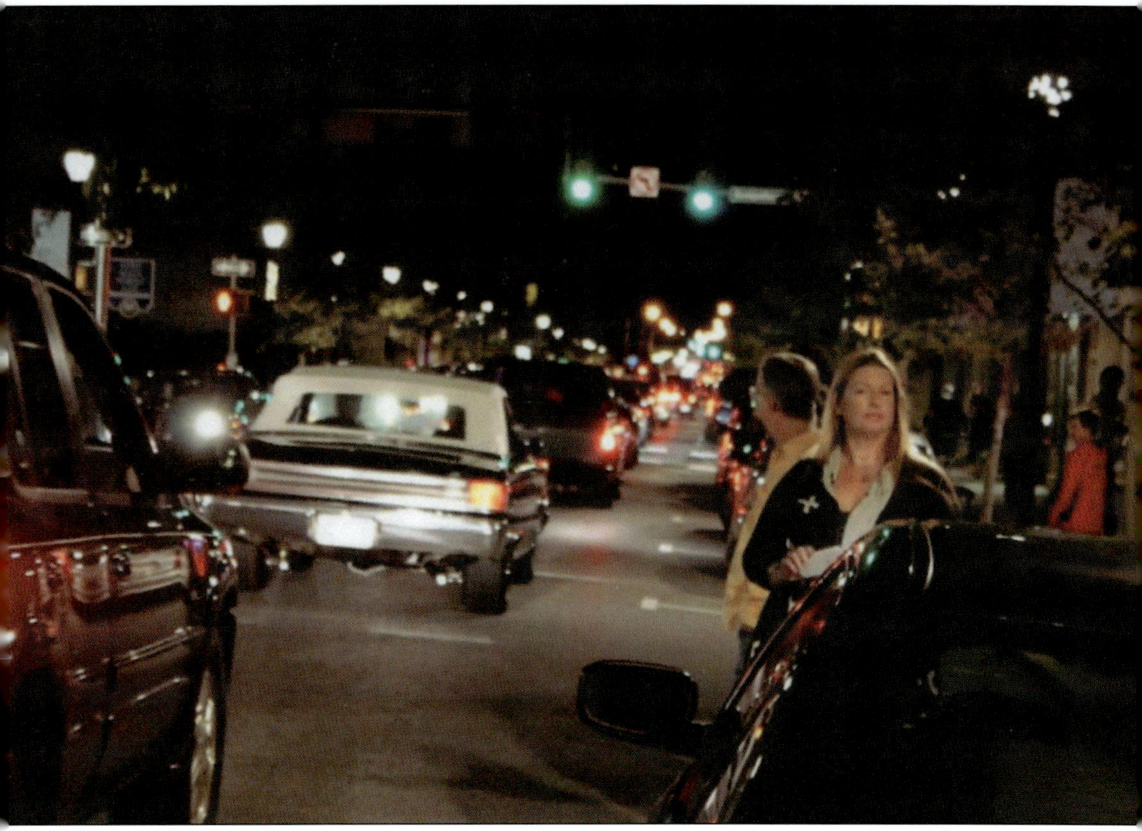

Lansdale Cruise Night packed the streets for its annual cruise on September 20, 2014. Cars from different Pennsylvania counties are driven around during this chance to cruise like they did in the old days. Some people have been cruising Lansdale for years, and others are new to the area. Many have passed on their love of the town and cruising to new generations. (Courtesy of Bill Salter.)

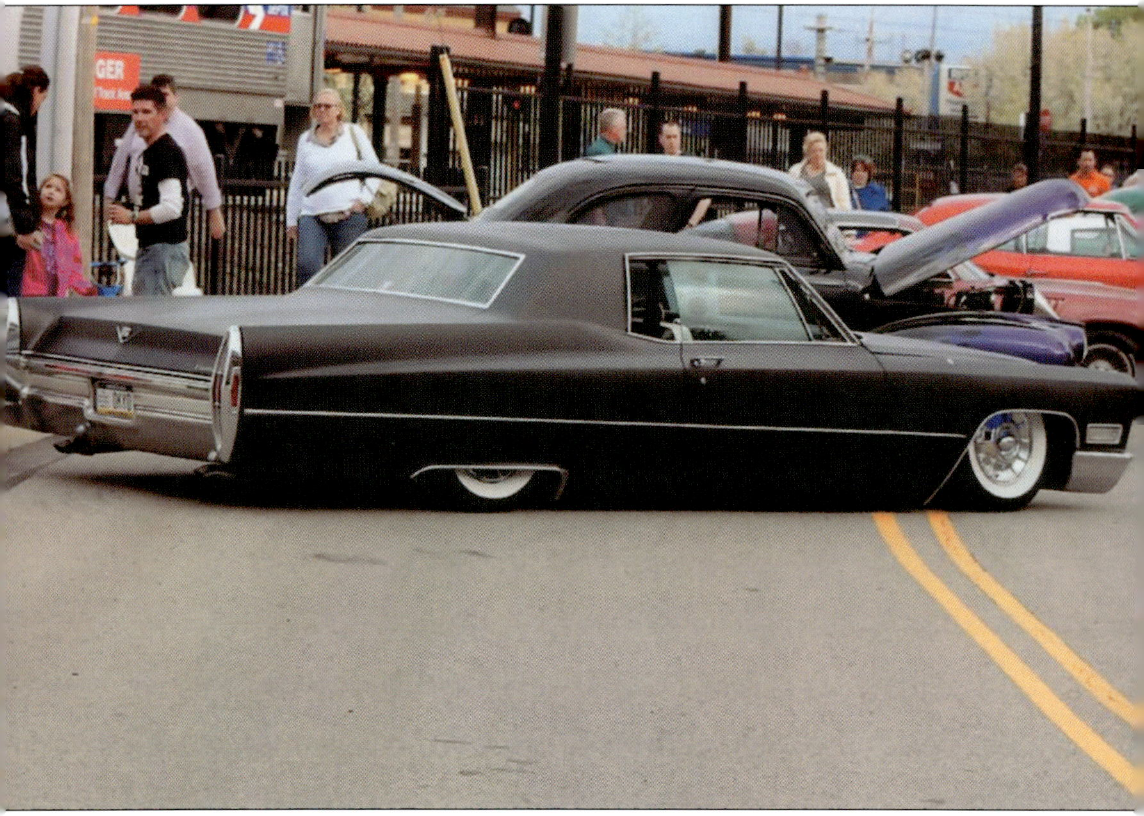

Lansdale cruisers had their first monthly night out on May 1, 2015, at an event called Lansdale First Friday. These cars are on display by the SEPTA station, and many stop to take pictures and find their favorite car or truck. Some people bring their children to share in their love of cruising and cars at this family-friendly event, which is held on the first Friday of each month. Trophies are given out by the sponsor, East Penn Modifiers Club. (Courtesy of Bill Salter.)

Two

Car and Bike Shows
Making Memories Count

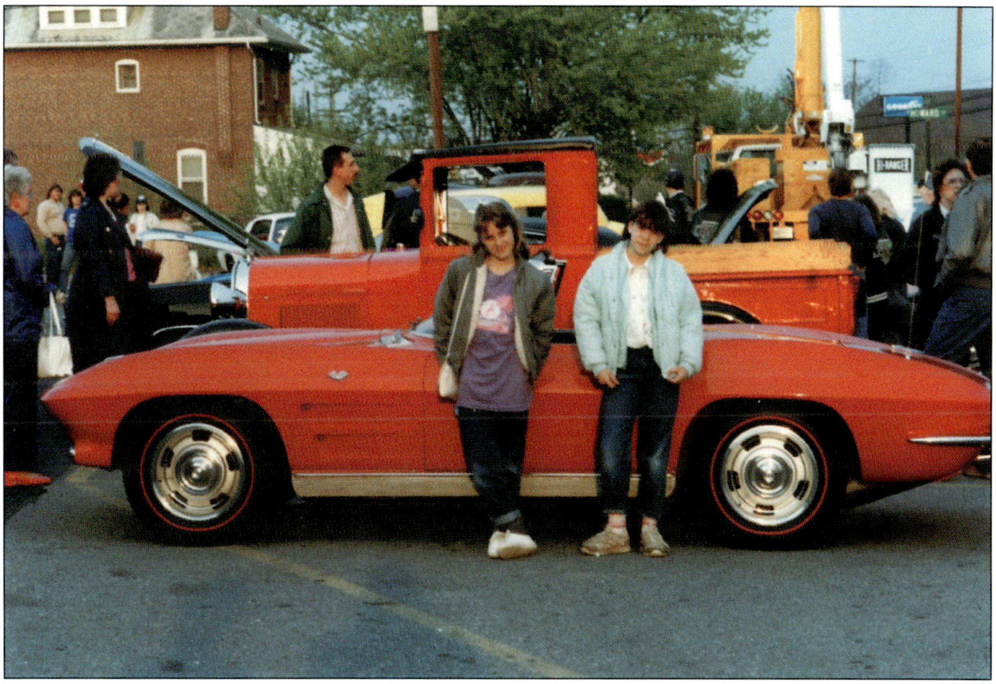

For many years, the Kutztown Fairgrounds Car Show was held in Berks County with over 400 cars on display. It featured live music, family fun, and vendors selling T-shirts, car parts, and food. The picture was taken in 1985 by Fred Spiezio, a race car driver and local master pyrotechnist. He has been taking pictures for many years at racetracks and car shows, capturing events in Montgomery and Berks Counties. (Courtesy of Fred Spiezio.)

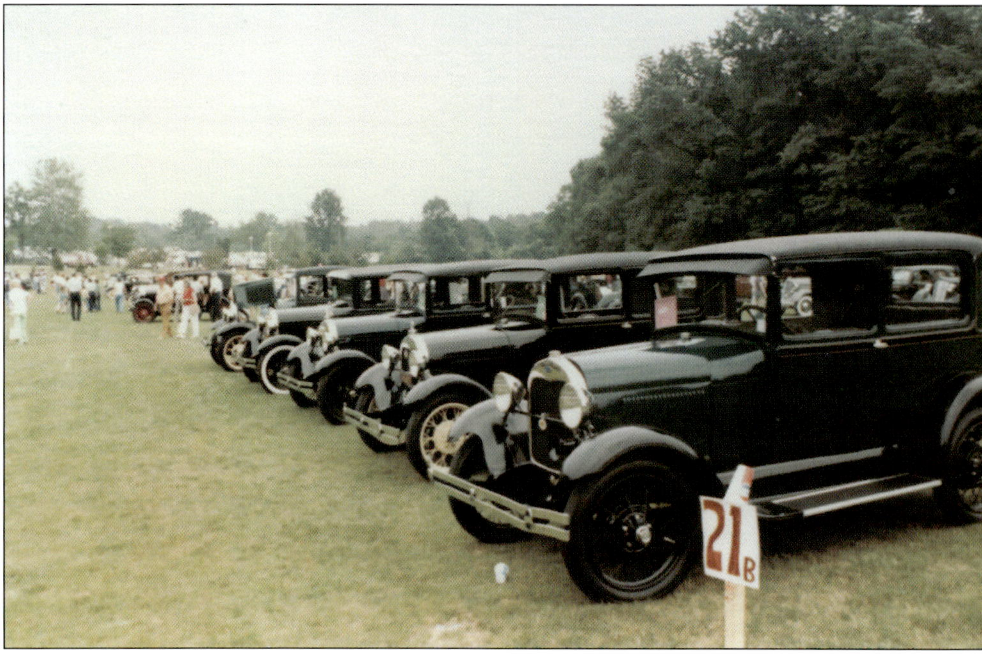

Penn State Berks Campus in Reading held an annual antique car show in the 1970s. It was presented for at least five years and always had a large amount of cars in each show. The show was part of a Spring Fair Day held by students to help raise money for their particular student groups. Tables were set up around the campus to encourage potential students to attend the school. Car enthusiasts of all ages attended the event, and many brought their families, too. (Both, courtesy of Fred Spiezio.)

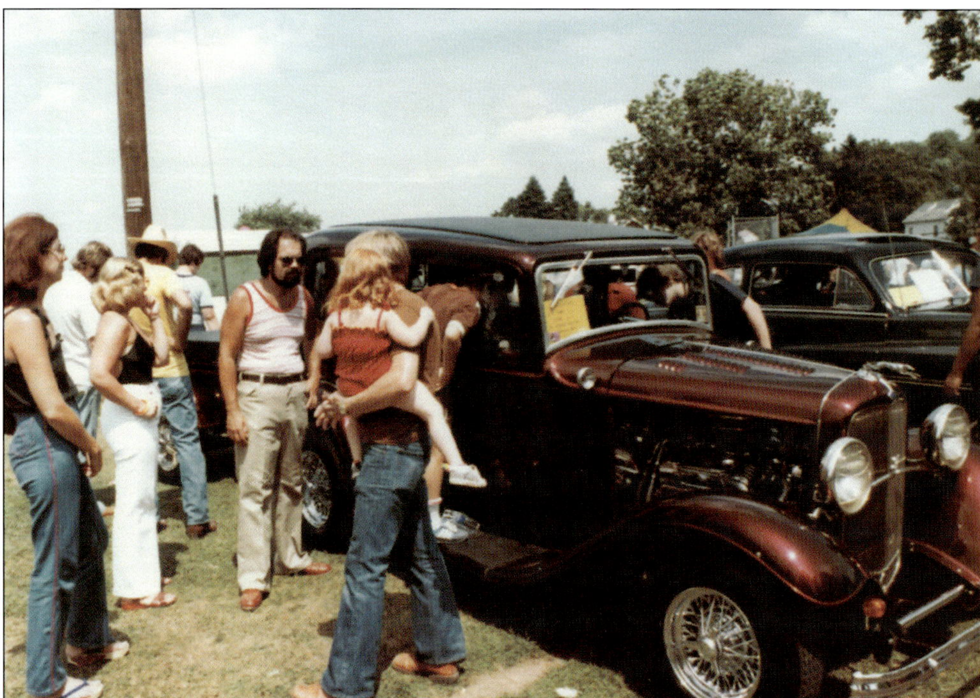

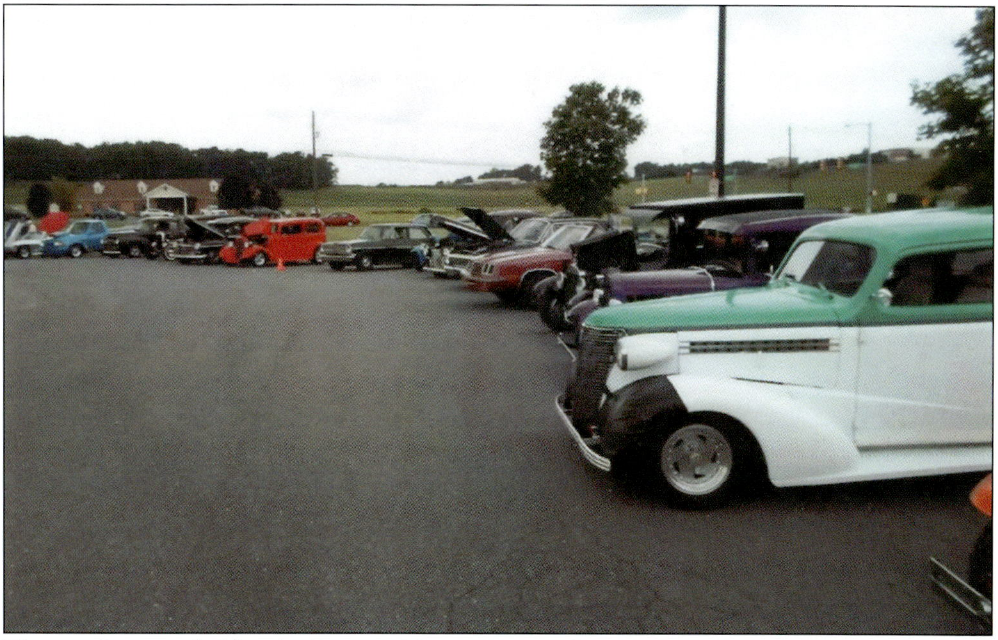

This car show was held at the Sonic in Morgantown on June 14, 2012. Car enthusiasts came from all over the area to show and to look at the amazing and fascinating cars and trucks on display. Pro street, muscle cars, and hot rods are displayed here every Thursday night. Morgantown is a beautiful area to drive through. (Courtesy of George Zlumlord Watters.)

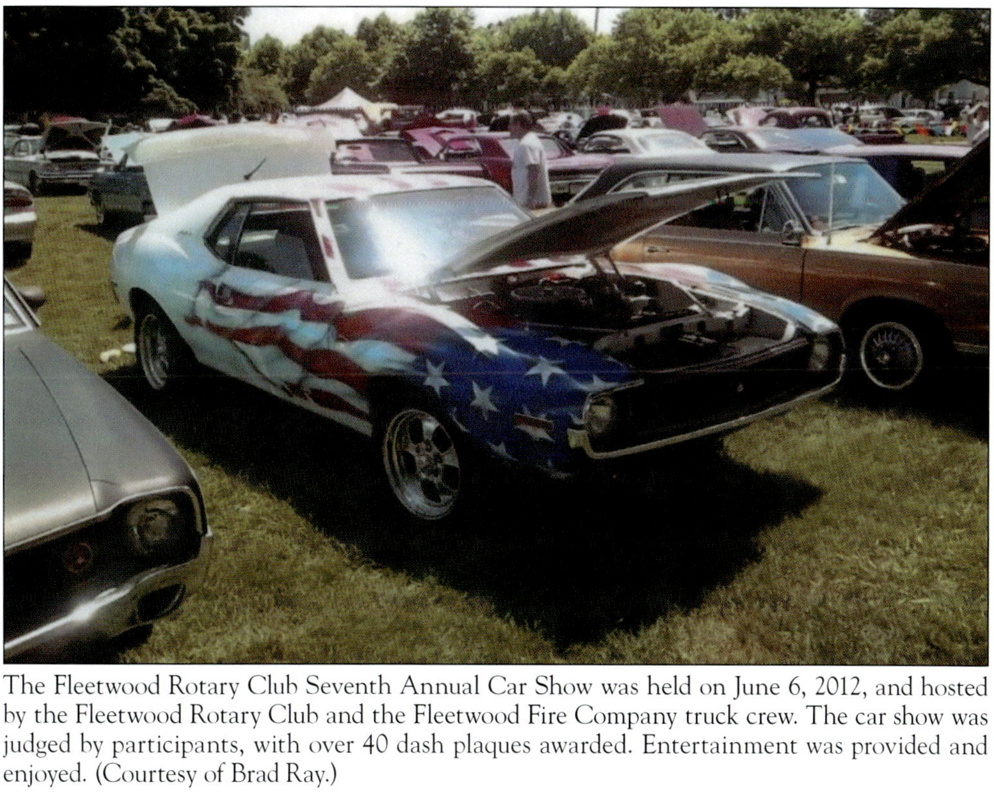

The Fleetwood Rotary Club Seventh Annual Car Show was held on June 6, 2012, and hosted by the Fleetwood Rotary Club and the Fleetwood Fire Company truck crew. The car show was judged by participants, with over 40 dash plaques awarded. Entertainment was provided and enjoyed. (Courtesy of Brad Ray.)

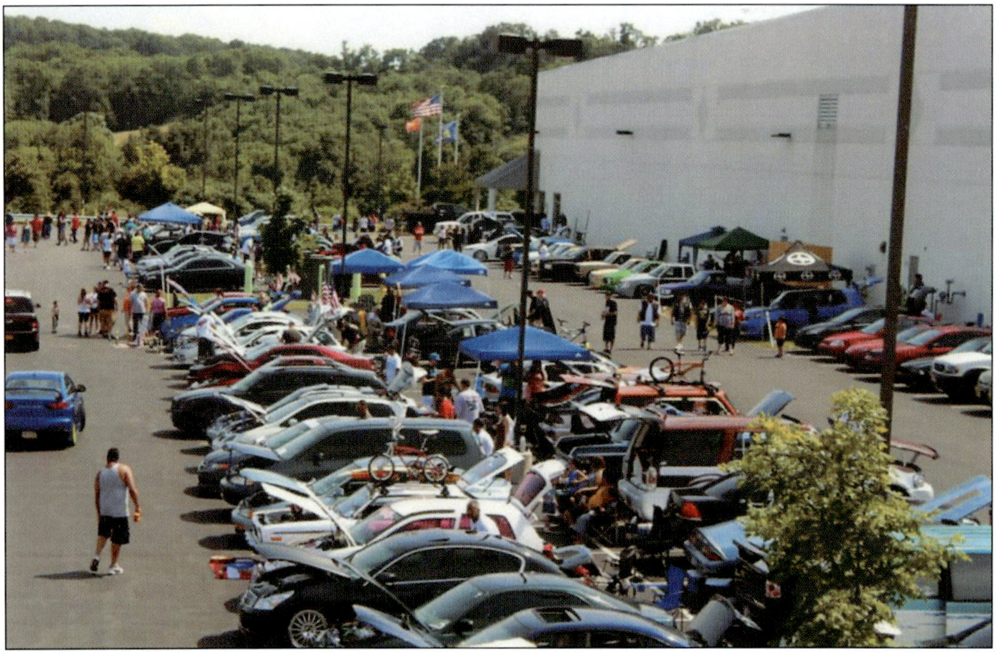

New Image Auto Club held this auto show on June 22, 2013, in Kutztown. The club was established in 1994 and has chapters throughout the region and in other states. It was established in New York City as a way to ease crime. The club has changed its name to Extreme Illusion Motorsports. (Courtesy of Bill Salter.)

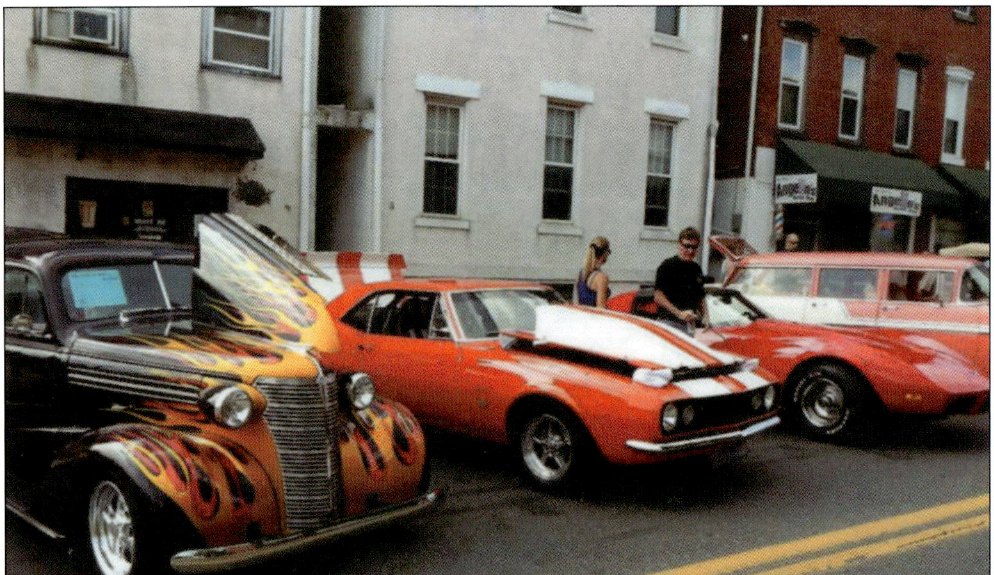

Building a Better Boyertown Seventh Annual Cruise Night was held on July 19, 2014, and sponsored by Wicked Car Effect and the Boyertown Museum of Historical Vehicles. Car enthusiasts traveled from far and wide to attend the event, and as many as 400 owners showcased their cars. Artists, charitable organizations, and vendors lined the streets for the fun-filled event. (Courtesy of Brad Ray.)

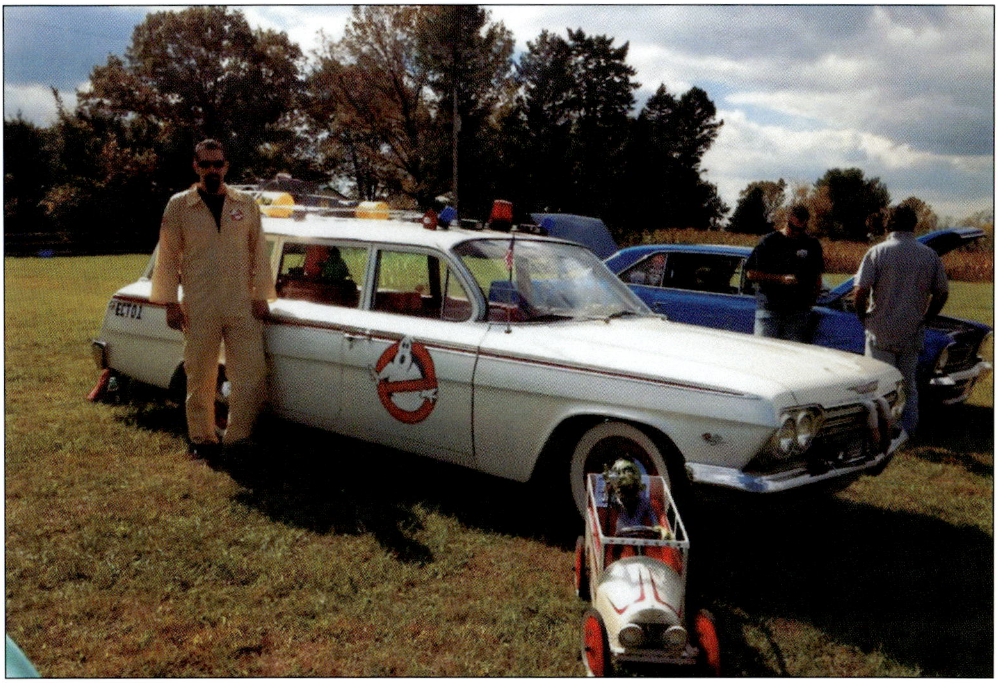

Justin Kulp attended the Pottstown Classics Car Club Pumpkin Run at Wilcox Farms with his station wagon designed in a *Ghostbusters* theme. It had a ghost inside, and Kulp himself dressed in a Ghostbuster outfit. Many were excited about his interesting car. (Courtesy of Justin Kulp.)

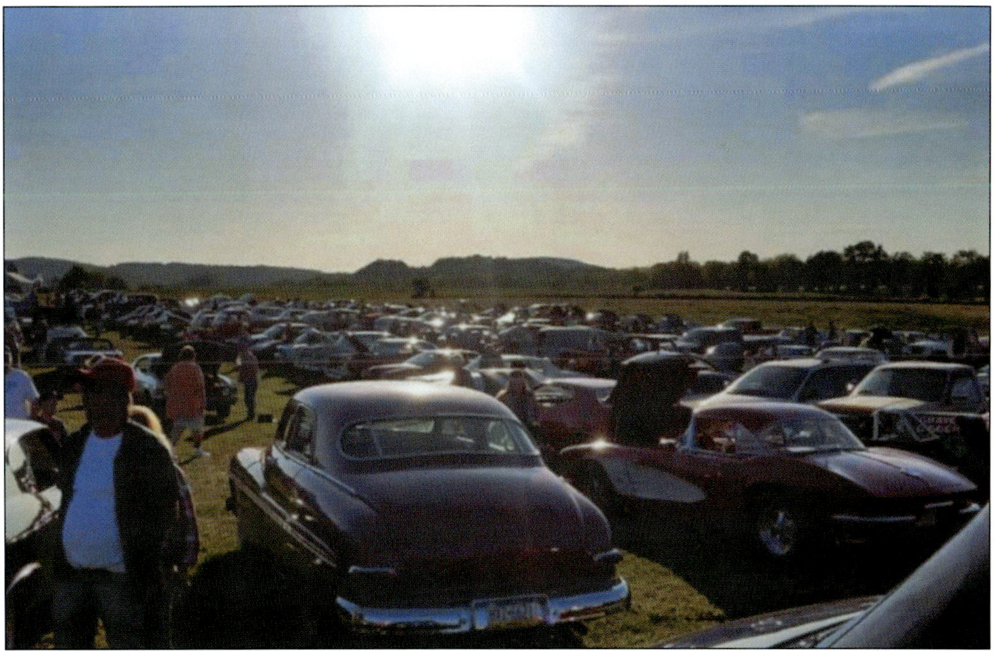

The Oley Turnpike Dairy hosts 12 shows per year, starting in April and ending in September. The dairy, located between Reading and Boyertown, has been hosting shows for 15 years. The event features free parking and door prizes. The dairy has really beautiful surroundings, with large fields of corn, and is a wonderful place to watch the sunset. (Courtesy of Brad Ray.)

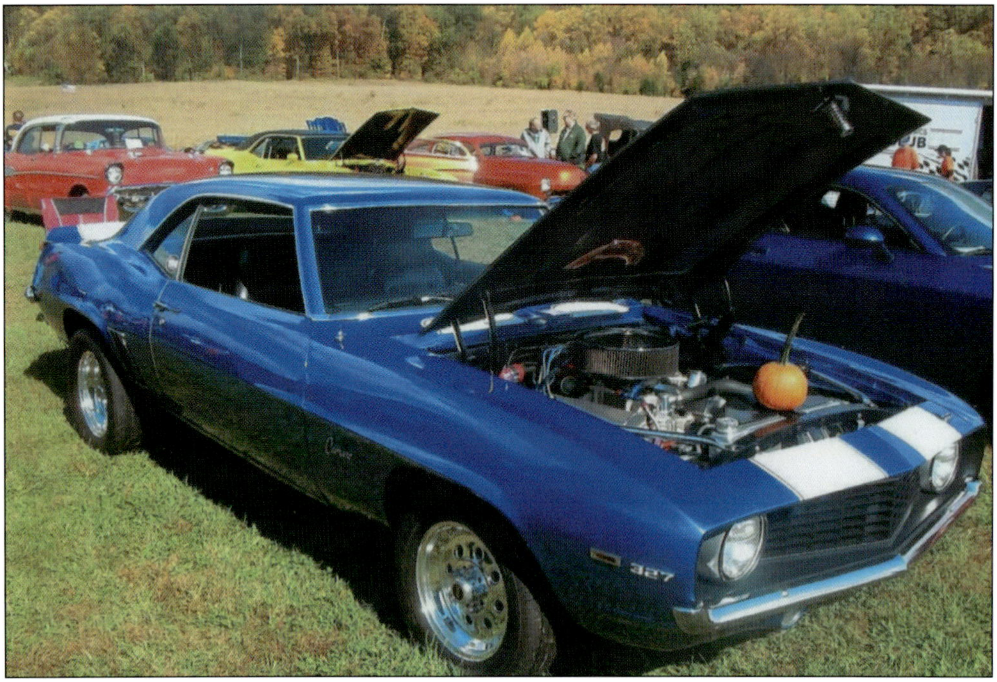

Pottstown Classics Car Club holds their annual Pumpkin Run at Wilcox Farms in Boyertown, Pennsylvania. The pictured event was held on October 18, 2014. Trophies were presented in 14 classes. Best of show was awarded to Willy Bertoti, who passed away in July 2014. Bertoti was an amazing auto shop teacher at Pottstown High School for many years, and the car club created the Willy Bertoti Memorial Scholarship Fund in his honor. (Courtesy of Jennifer Bowen.)

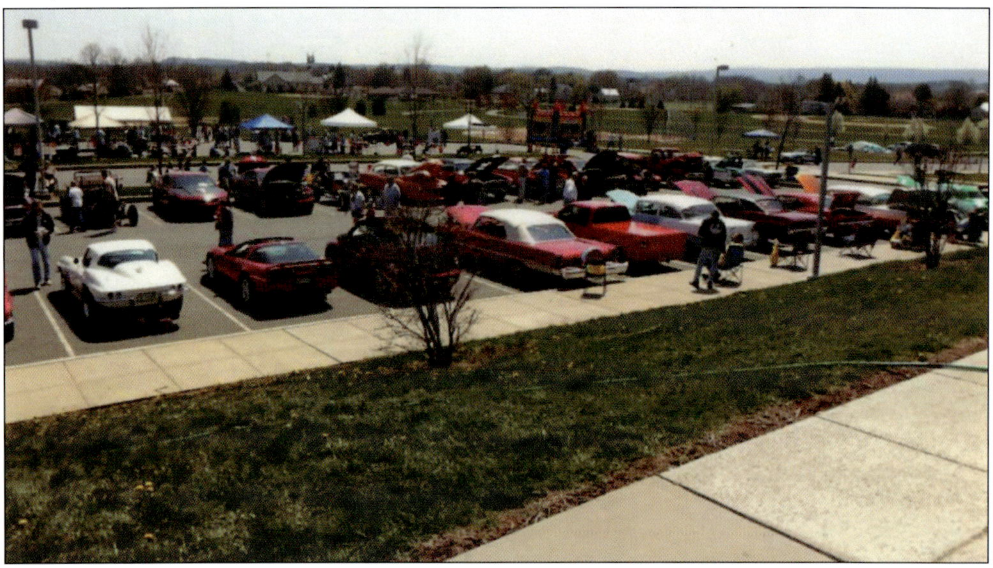

Boy Scout Troop 597 of Amityville, Pennsylvania, held its Seventh Annual Antique & Classic Car Show and Community Carnival on April 26, 2014. The show was held at Daniel Boone Middle School. Trophies were given out in nine categories, including best in show and overall Scouts' choice. Many people try to get into this show early since it has a large turnout. (Courtesy of Brad Ray.)

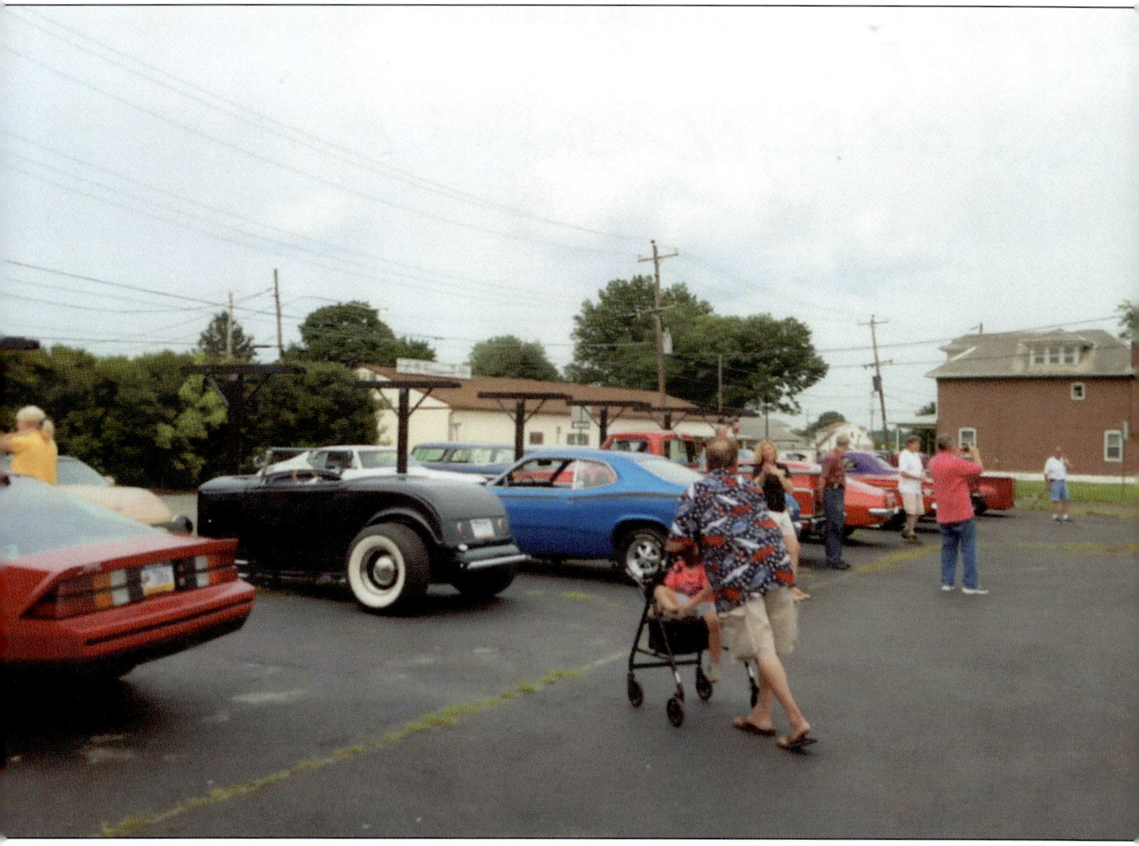

The "Good old days of Pottstown! Then and Now" Facebook group held its first annual cruise and car show on July 3, 2015. The show was at Hilltop Drive-In and continued with a cruise down High Street in Pottstown. People came out to wave and take photographs of the long line of cruisers that day. The cars proceeded on to the former Philips Drive-In, also known as the Tropical Treat. Many people stayed to reminisce about the old days at the drive-in. After about two hours, a few people decided to cruise over to the former Rocks Diner on Route 100. It was a day full of delightful memories. (Courtesy of Tina Kissinger.)

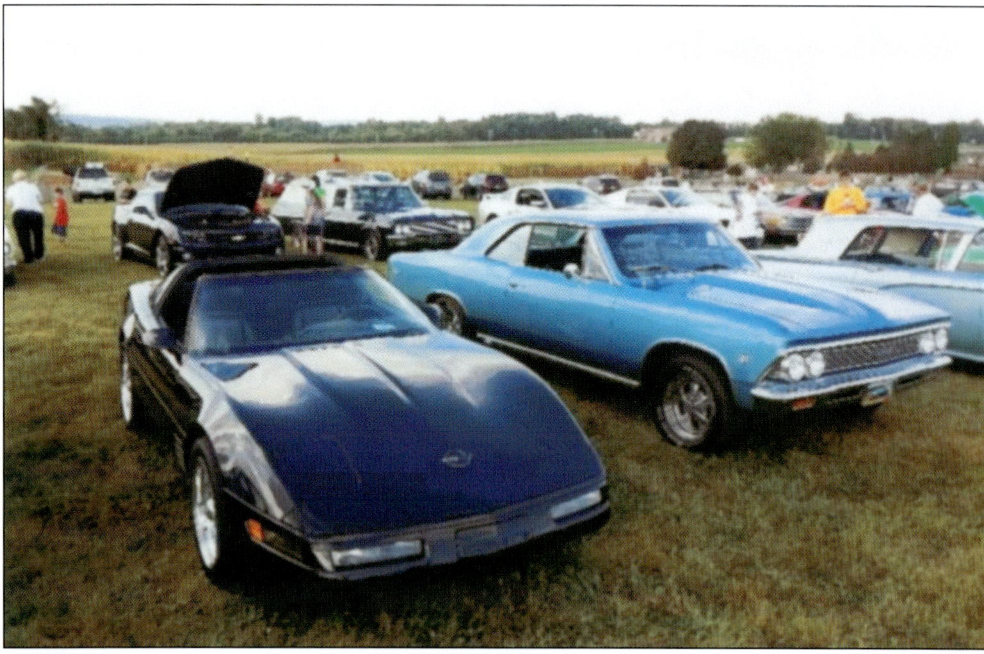

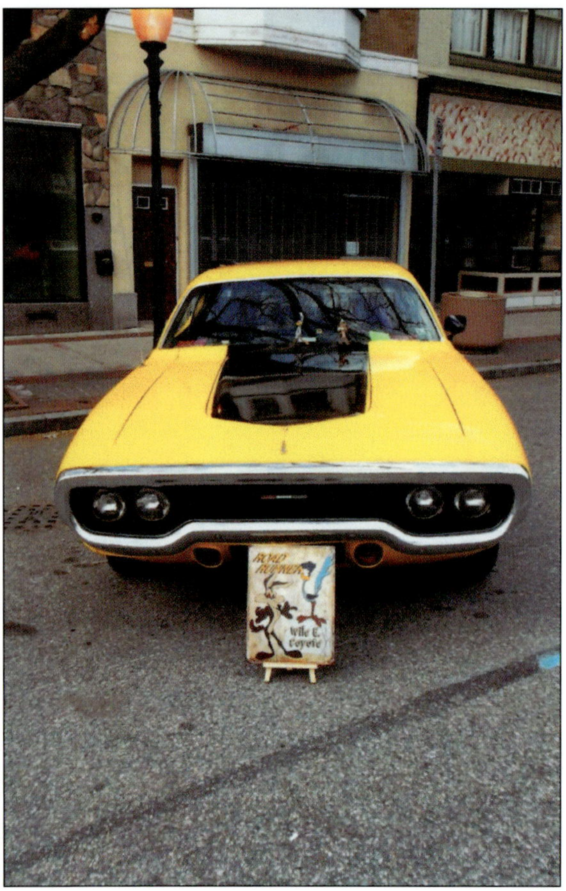

Oley Turnpike Dairy holds an annual cruise night. Many awards, including Ladies' Night and Best in Show, were given out at the 2015 event. This car show is a great for families, as the dairy has a petting zoo and a nice restaurant with excellent food and ice cream to help create a wonderful outing. (Courtesy of Brad Ray.)

Ed Admaski of Pottstown cruised around in his 1971 Plymouth Road Runner on High Street in the 1970s and 1980s. Admaski always said his first Plymouth Road Runner saved his life during an accident. If he ever found a new one, he would buy it. He now attends car shows around the area in his new Plymouth, for which he has won several trophies. (Courtesy of Charlene Franey-Stein.)

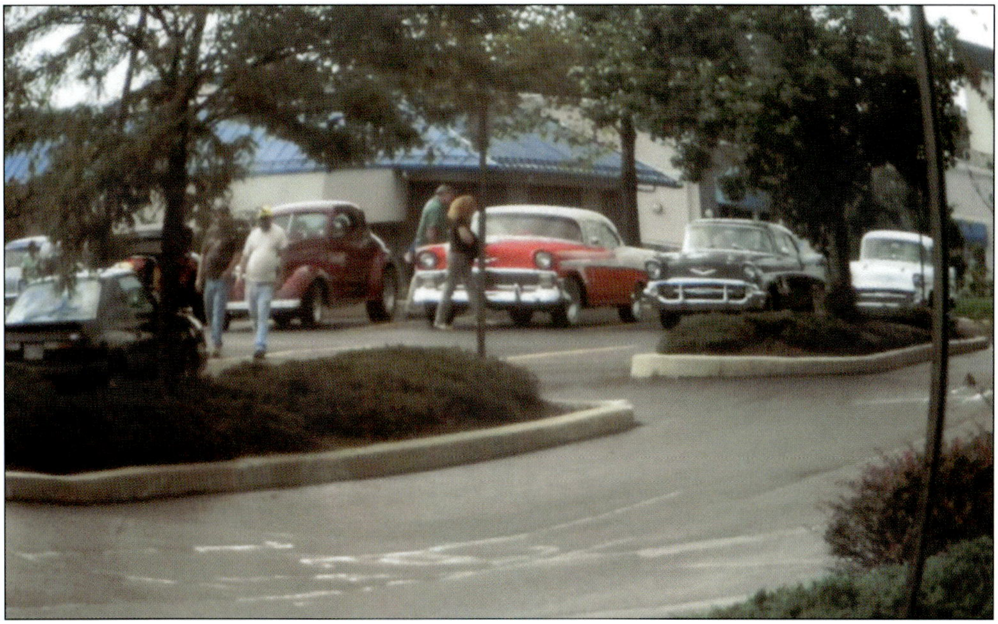

The Moonlight Memories Car Show is held in Hatboro, located in Montgomery County. This photograph shows the event held in July 2010. The annual car show is still held on the last Saturday of July each year. In 2015, the car show celebrated its 23rd year, and more than 75,000 car enthusiasts come out to support their hobby and cruise. Cars—including classic, antique, Pro Street, sports cars, motorcycles, trucks, and vans—filled the streets and crossed over Moreland Avenue. (Courtesy of Bill Salter.)

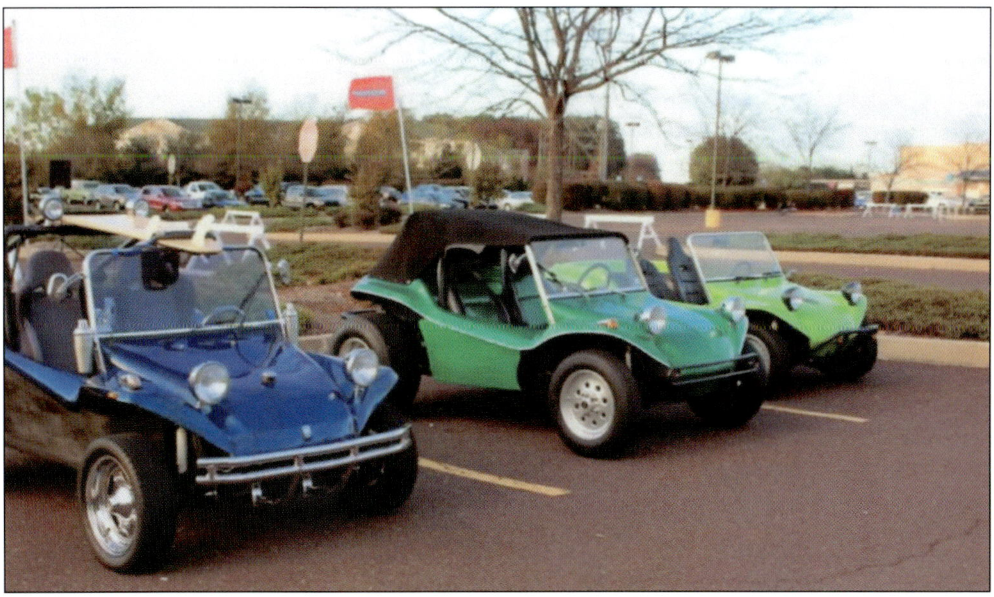

This cruise night, hosted by Bucks Mont Street Machine, was held in the Walmart parking lot in Harleysville in April 2013. It featured a variety of motorcycles, cars, and trucks, including the buggies pictured. People come from several parts of eastern Pennsylvania to attend this event, which has been running for over 30 years. It originally started in Montgomeryville, in the Marshall's parking lot on Main Street, near North Wales. (Courtesy of Bill Salter.)

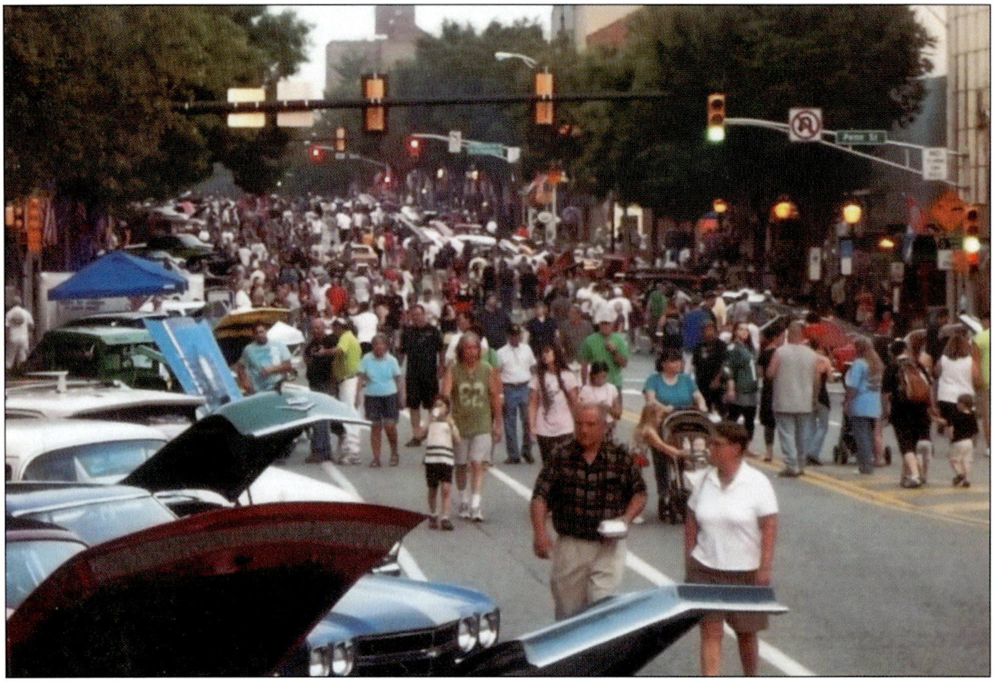

A crowd strolls down High Street in Pottstown, Pennsylvania on July 2011. Beautiful classic cars are on display on High and Charlotte Streets, and everyone is enjoying the relaxed event celebrating Pottstown's pastime. Food vendors and local restaurants serve hot dogs, funnel cake, French fries, and their best dishes to a hungry crowd. (Courtesy of Brad Ray.)

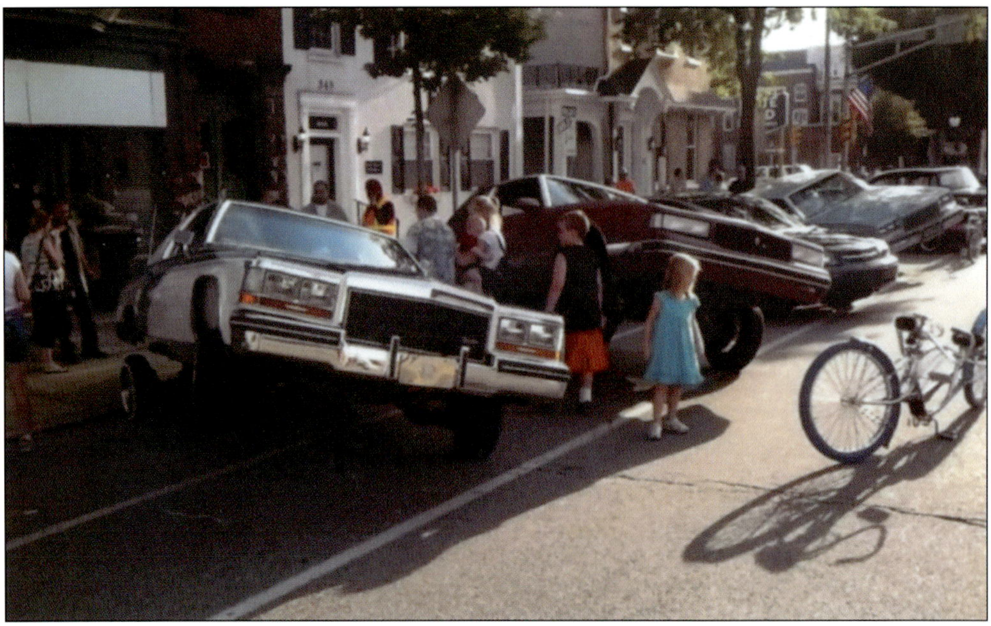

Pottstown Classics Car Club's Nostalgia Nights Car Show on July 2, 2011, presented amazing and exciting cars, and the crowd had a chance to see how much participants enjoy their hobby. Pottstown residents and visitors are well known for their love of cars on High Street and put a lot of money into their vehicles. (Courtesy of Brad Ray.)

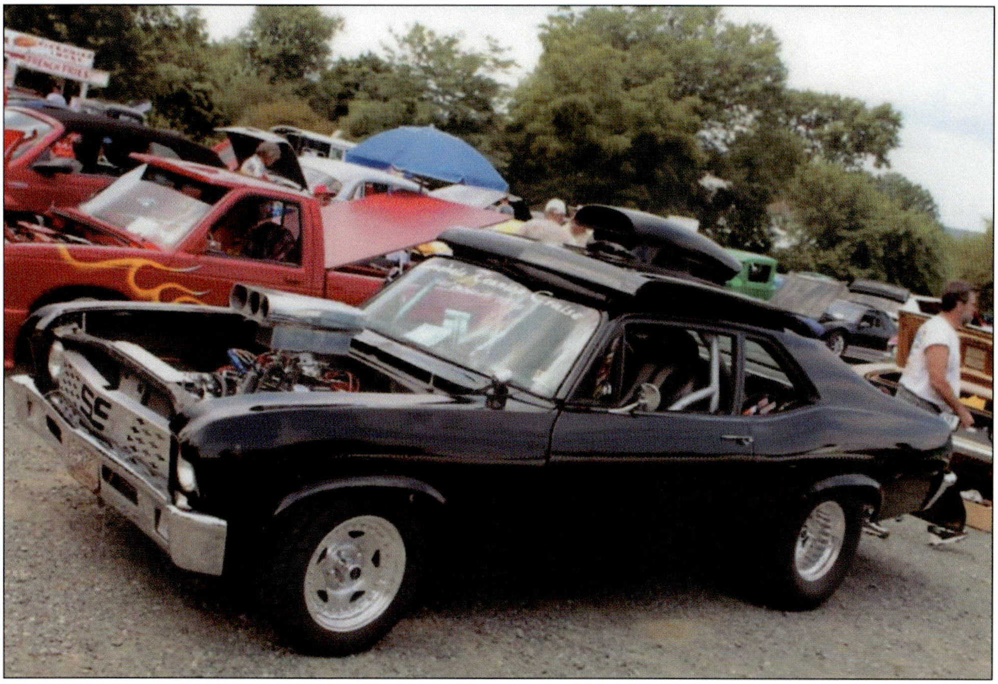

A car show named Cruize for a Cure was held on May 11, 2013, in Gilbertsville, Pennsylvania. Miracles from Him Relay for Life sponsored this event, and Rubright Racing Enterprises gave out trophies in 16 categories. A new location for this event has been established at Morning Star Fellowship in Bechtelsville. (Courtesy of Bill Salter.)

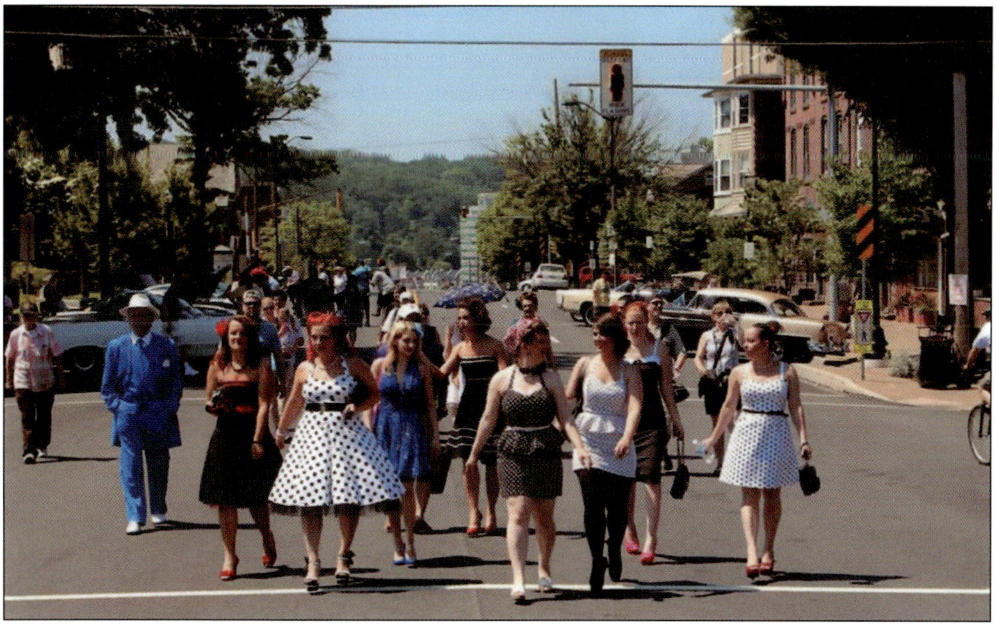

Conshohocken Car Show held this pin-up pageant during their 12th annual car show on Fayette Street, with the show lasting from 9:00 a.m. to 3:00 p.m. The pageant is a popular event held at many car shows. The winner receives a crown and sash. People often take photographs of the ladies modeling in the cars. (Courtesy of Bill Salter.)

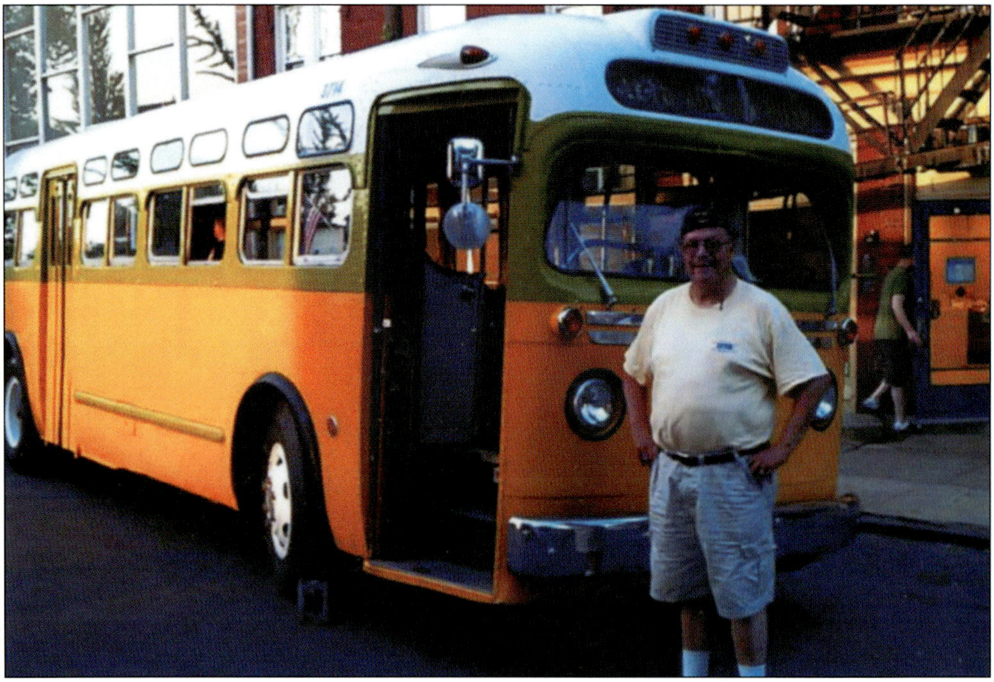

Glenn Ray posed with his friend Tom Kane's bus at the Pottstown Classics Car Club show on June 1, 2013. The bus is a 1956 model made by General Motors. It was originally in service in Oklahoma City and owned by the City Bus Company. Eventually, it was put in a junkyard for scrap but was restored. This bus is taken to different car and truck shows, and it is always very popular among the crowd. (Courtesy of Brad Ray.)

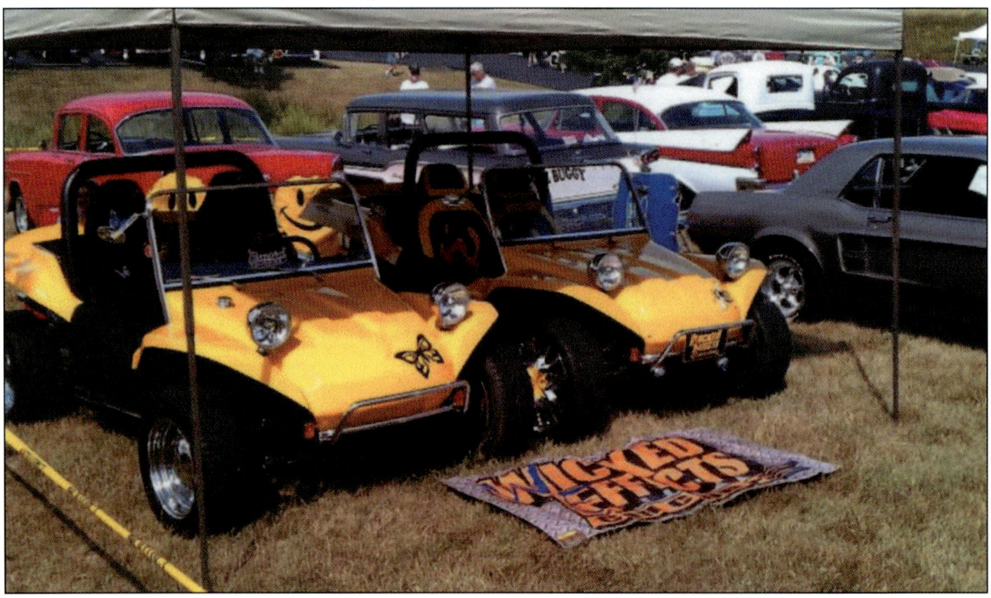

The Eastwood Company car show was held in Pottstown on July 14, 2012. Eastwood Company holds a car show each year. Many people from all over the area attend this large show. Different classes of vehicles are on display, including custom vans. Penny and Elvis's dune buggies are shown here, along with a banner from Wicked Car Effects Car Club. (Courtesy of Brad Ray.)

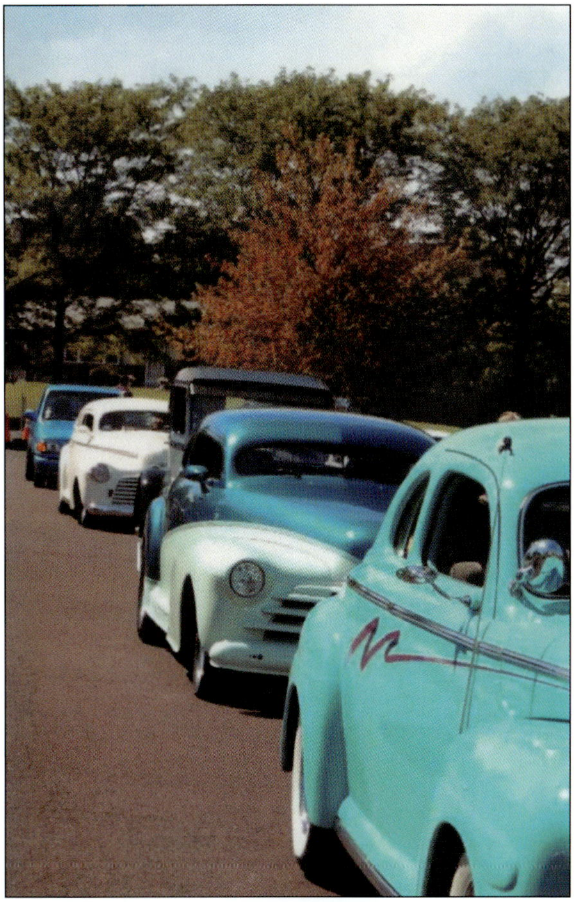

New Hanover United Methodist Church, located on Swamp Pike in Gilbertsville, held an annual Classic Car & Bike Show on September 15, 2014. The show benefits Happy 2 Be Home, and music, food, awards, and prizes are provided. (Courtesy of New Hanover Methodist Church.)

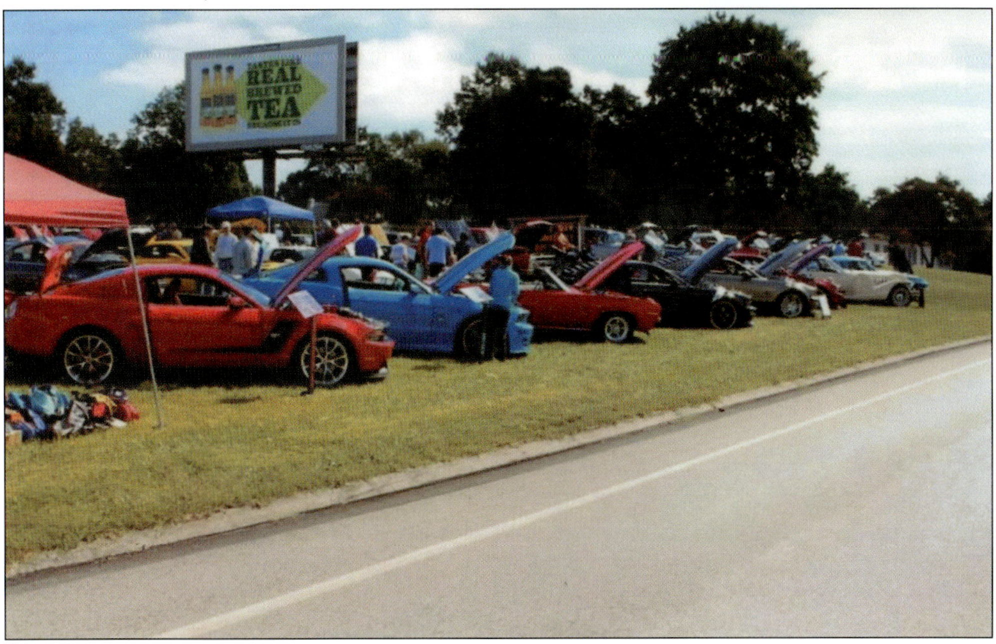

In 2014, the Full House Motorsports car show was held at Providence Fire Company in Montgomery County. The show was run by Brian Lutz, Bill Salter, and Jimmy Dorris. They had an amazing turnout. Steve Shatten, Nicole Shatten, Rick Schreiter, John Soloman, Eric Hawk, Kevin Wolbach, and Rick Schreiter displayed their cars in the front row. (Courtesy of Bill Salter.)

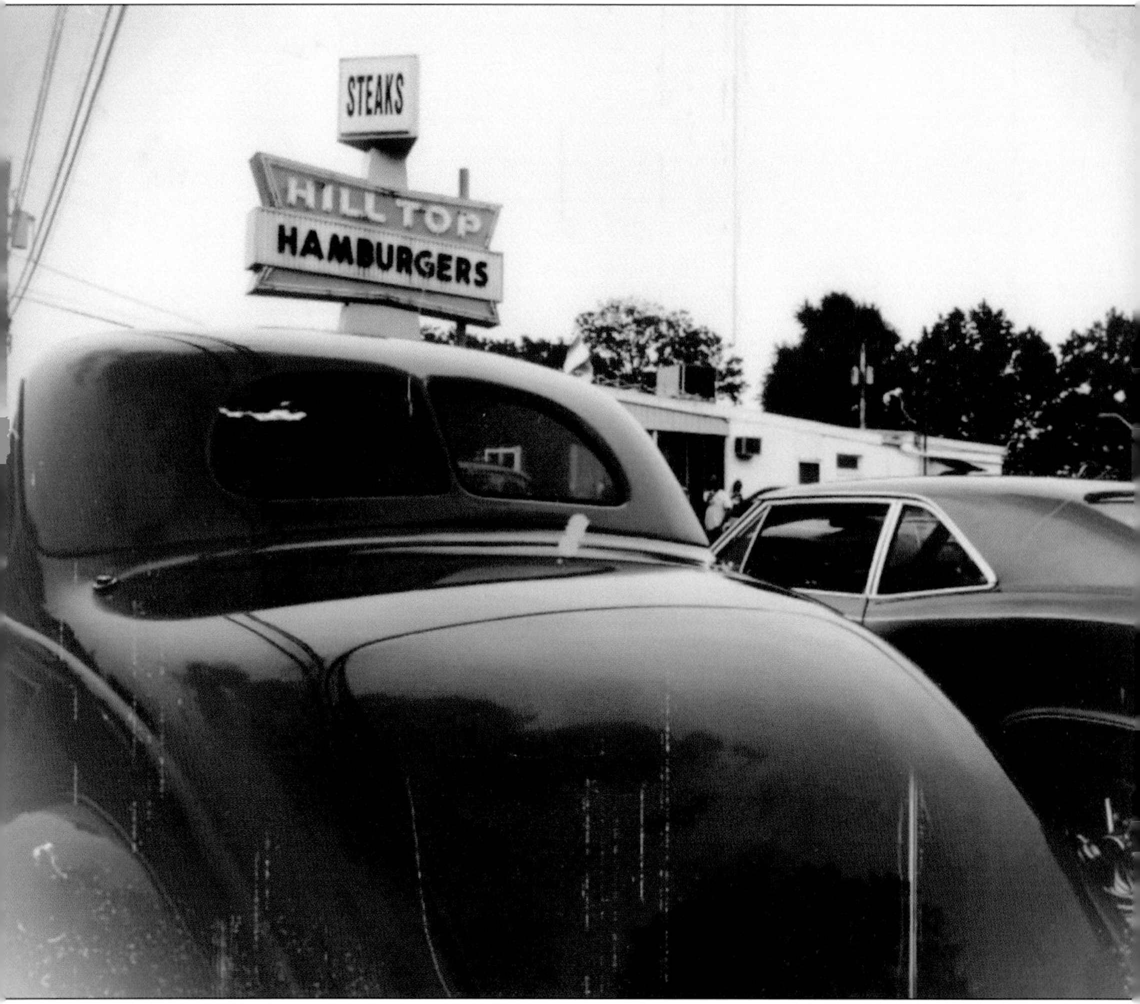

Hilltop Drive-In, located at 2910 East High Street in Pottstown, cohosted the "Good old days of Pottstown! Then and Now" Facebook page cruise on July 3, 2015. It was open to the public, with or without a car. As many as 150 cars were there, along with many people catching up with everyone. They enjoyed a nice meal, bought T-shirts, and later cruised High Street. The parking lot and restaurant were packed. The members of "Good old days of Pottstown! Then and Now" hope to host more car shows. (Courtesy of George Zlumlord Watters.)

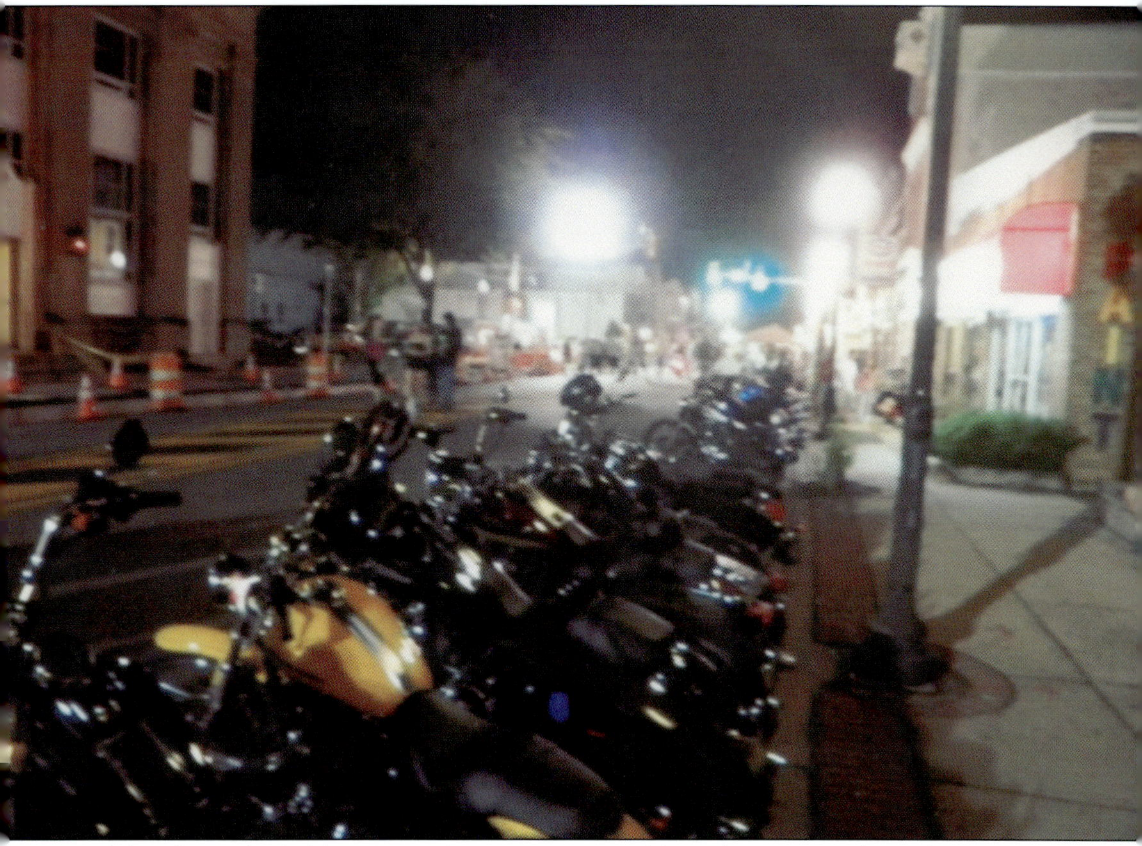

Lansdale Bike Night, held on September 6, 2014, was celebrated at Main and Broad Streets in Lansdale. This is one of the largest one-night bike nights in the country. Trophies are given to several classes of vehicles, including Radical Choppers, stock motorcycles, Iron Head Sporters, sport bikes, sidecars, trucks, and many more. The event was sponsored by Blue Comet Motorcycle Club and featured vendors, music, and food. (Courtesy of George Zlumlord Watters.)

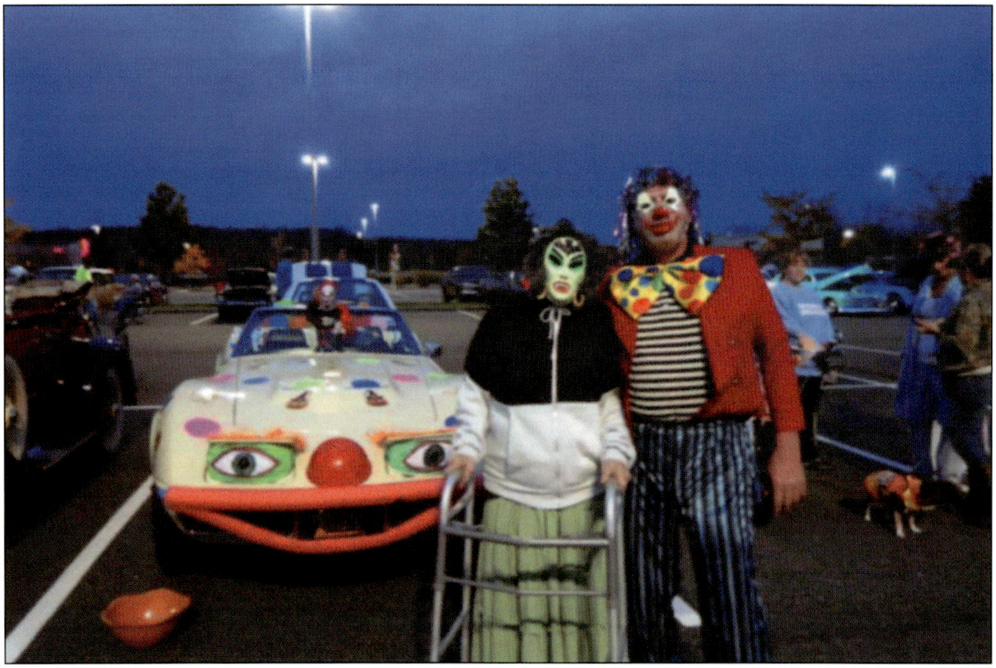

This Wicked Effects Car Club show was held in October 2014 at Carmike Theatre in Upland Square in Pottstown. The club's Halloween show is always a big event. Here, Andrew Bealer Sr. and his mother, Grace Bealer, are dressed for the occasion, and their Corvette is decorated, too. Wicked Effects Car Club was established in 2008. (Courtesy of Andrew Bealer.)

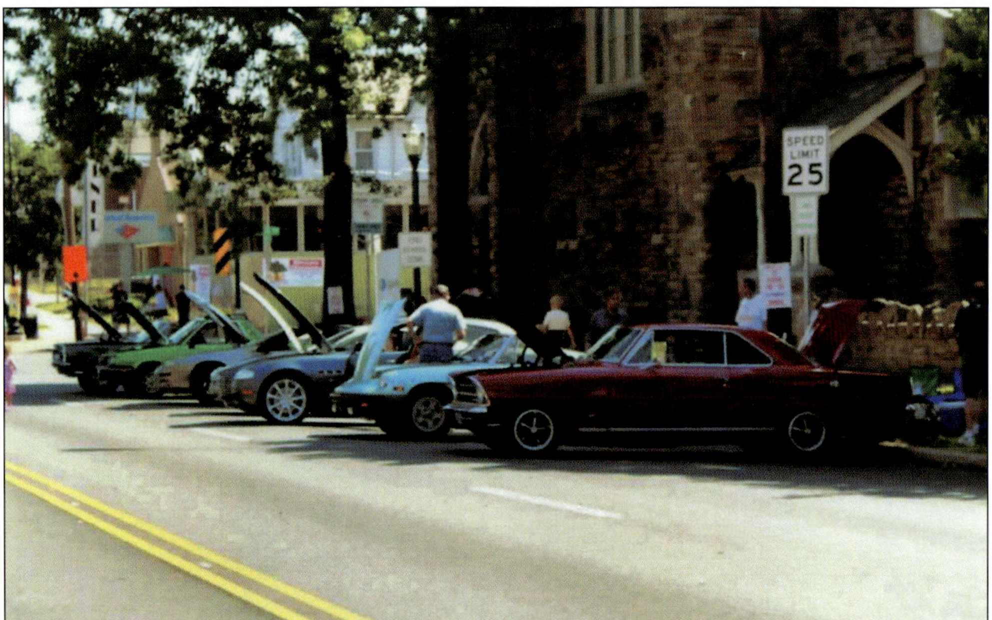

Conshohocken's Special Events Committee sponsored the 12th annual car show on Saturday, June 1, 2013. They gave out over 60 trophies for motorcycles, trucks, classic cars, and exotic models. The event featured a disc jockey, food vendors, raffles, T-shirts for sale, and special guests. (Courtesy of Bill Salter.)

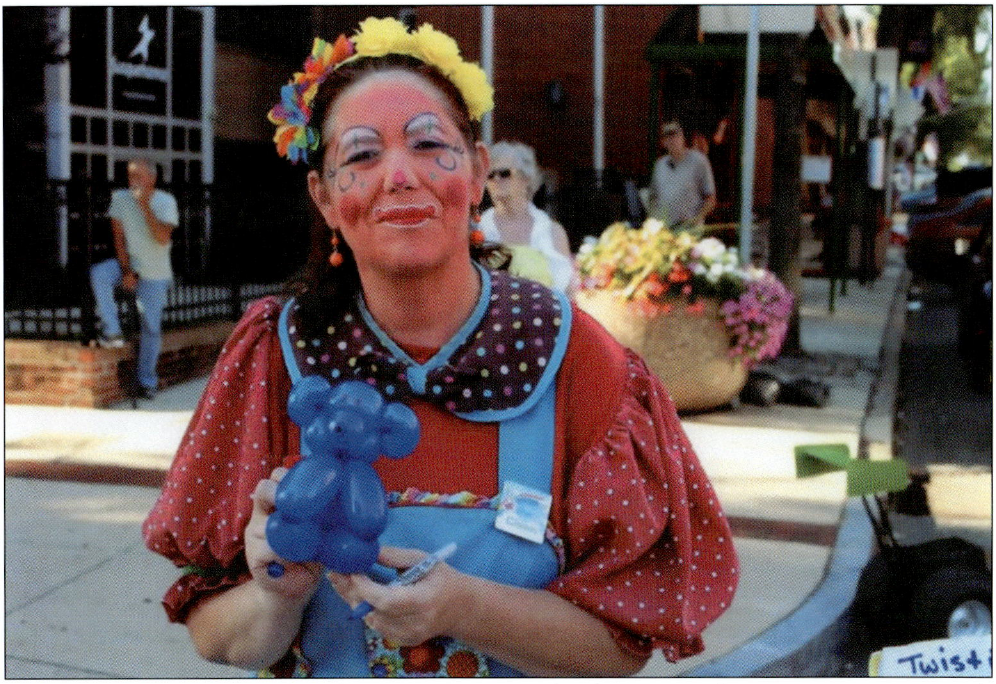

Here, Rainbow the Clown (also known as Denise Perkins)—an award-winning entertainer with 13 years of experience—makes balloon animals for children and adults at a Pottstown Classics Car Club event in 2015. She is often found entertaining crowds at various shows throughout the region. Children look forward to watching her amaze the crowd with her creations. This event also featured fantasy face painting, magic shows, and much more. (Courtesy of Brad Ray.)

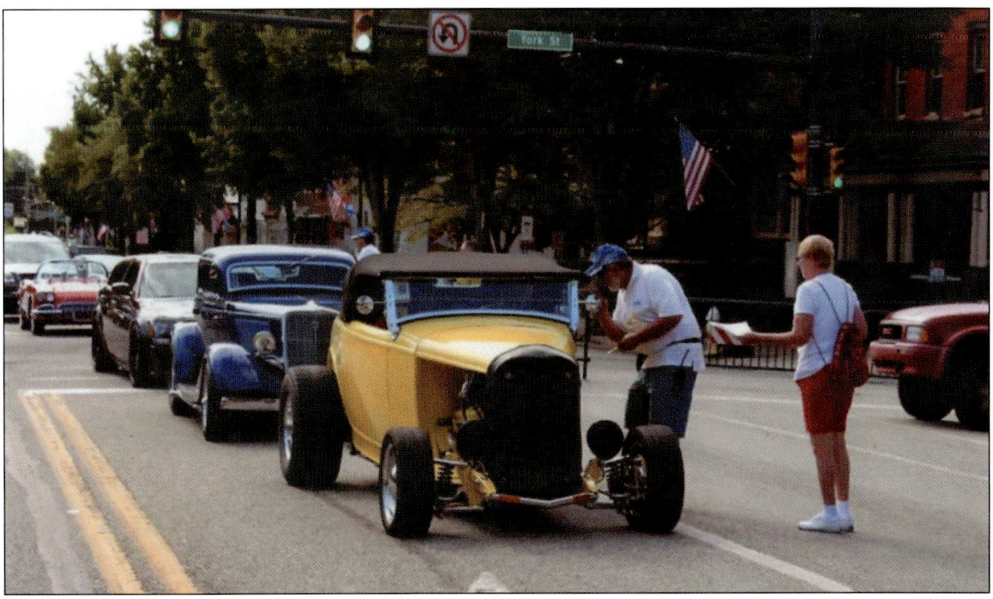

Biney Lawhorne helps register and park cars at the Pottstown Classics Car Club's summer 2015 car show. It takes several members and volunteers to help with this event; luckily, they all enjoy being involved with the club and this hobby. Each year, the club selects a charity to donate money to so the club can give back to the community. (Courtesy of Brad Ray.)

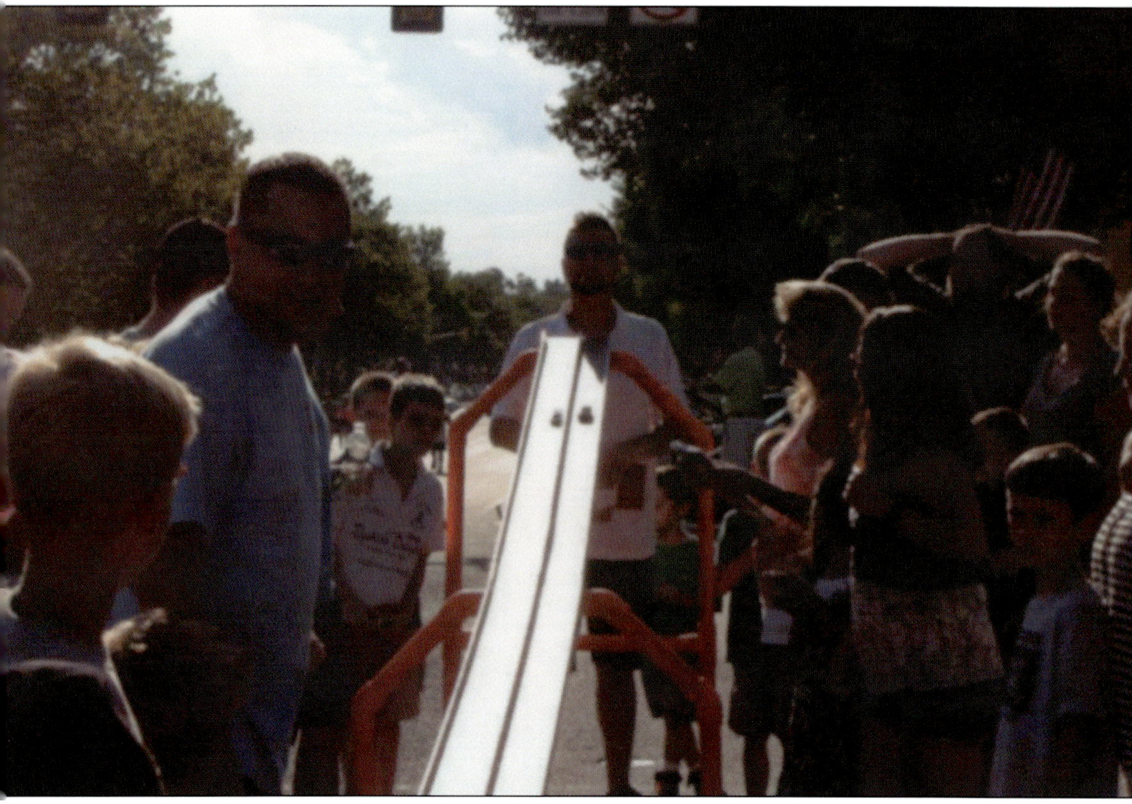

Brad Ray, of Pottstown Classics Car Club, facilitates the Hot Wheels competition for children as part of the August 3, 2015, car show. The children look forward to this event, and three winners are awarded trophies. A crowd always gathers around to see who will win. (Courtesy of Brad Ray.)

Actor Brett "Big Schwag" Wagner (far left in the image at right), known for his role on *Sons of Anarchy*, as host of *Monster Garage*, and as a syndicated radio host and producer, attends the Northeast Rod & Custom Car Show, which was held on March 21–23, 2013. He is calibrating with Montgomery County Technical Career Center students on the Schwag Project, for which students built a Mustang with auto-shop teacher Bob Hunter. Car enthusiasts traveled from around the country to visit this indoor car show. (Courtesy of Bill Salter.)

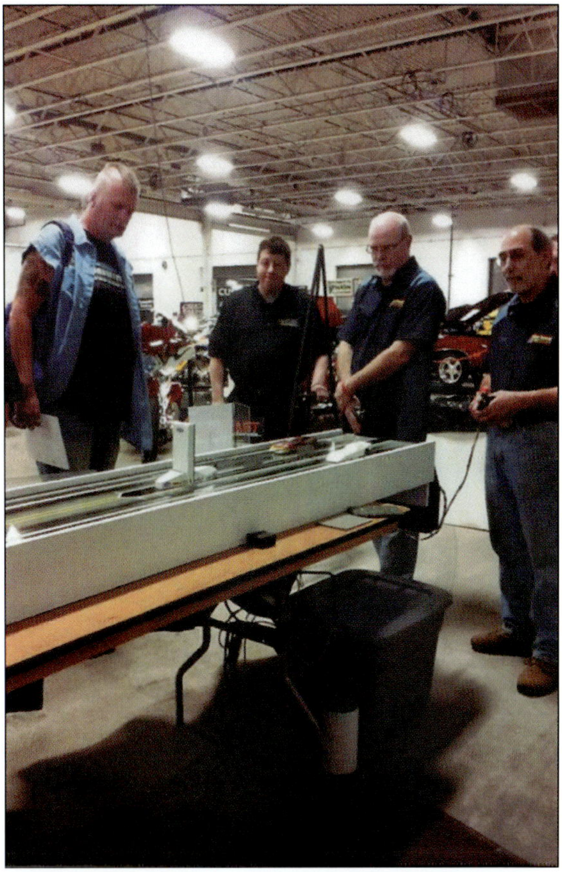

The Annual Royersford Community Day & Car Show was held on September 6, 2014. Cars lined Main Street for about a half-mile stretch in Royersford. Cars and trucks were shown from all classes. The event also featured a pet show, street performers, crafters, live music, and games. Crowds at this event have been growing; 4,000 people attended in 2013. Trophies and awards were given in many categories. (Courtesy of Fred Spiezio.)

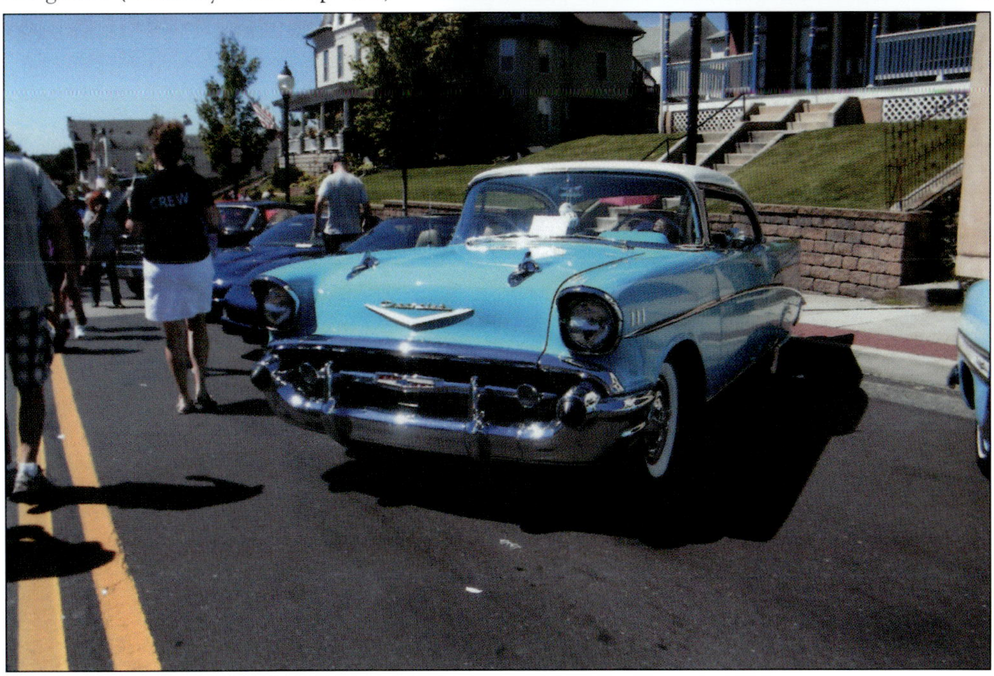

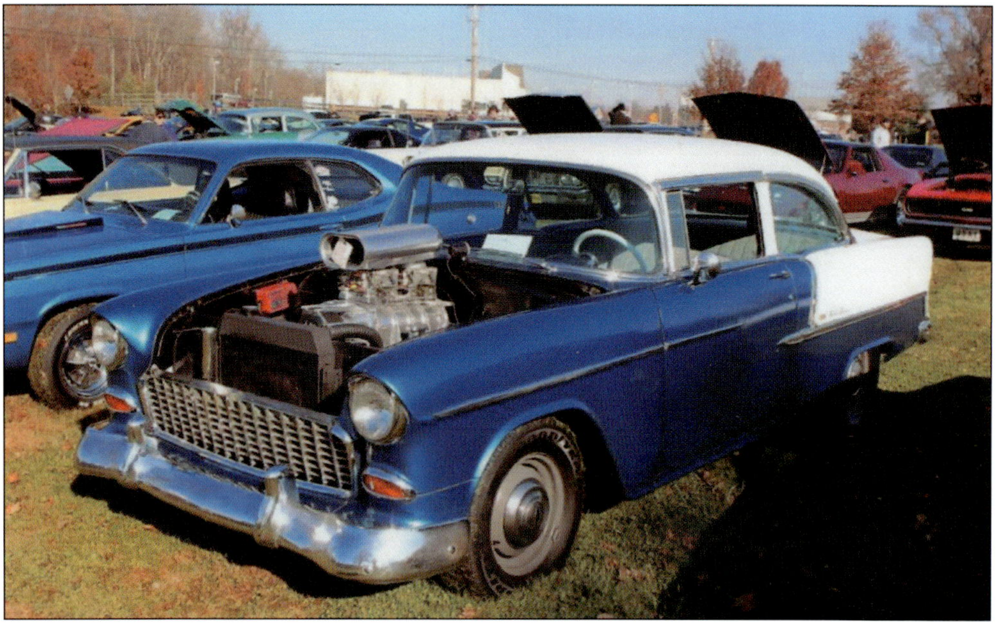

James Beagle's 1955 Chevy is pictured here at Rubright Racing Enterprises & Pottstown Classics Car Club Benevolent Car Show. At this benefit show for April Grim and her family, participants were asked to bring Christmas gifts for two boys and three girls. Cars and trucks from different classes were present, with awards given in each category. A 50-50 raffle was held, and plenty of money was raised to help the family in need. (Courtesy of Mark Rubright.)

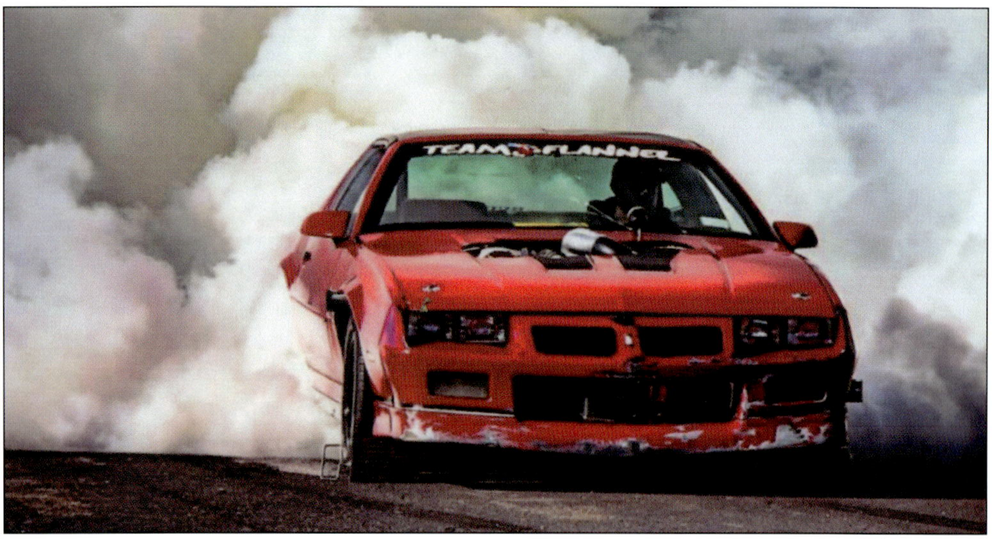

Paul Guerre-Chaley Jr. of Boyertown won first place during the burnout contest at the fifth annual Rubright Racing Enterprises/Pottstown Classics Car Club benefit show on November 21, 2015. Wicked Effects Car Club helped facilitate the burnout contest—a very popular event each year. Participants love to show the power of their car or truck. Fans gather around to watch the smoke and hear the tires squeal. Guerre-Chaley Jr. has a 1986 IROC-Z small-block Chevy with 355 engine and twin turbos. The car was a project that Guerre-Chaley Jr. and his father, Paul Guerre-Chaley Sr., decided to complete together. It was Guerre-Chaley Jr.'s first win, and he received $400 and a trophy. (Courtesy of Jerry Keefer of Keefer Photography.)

Three

Maple Grove Raceway
Life in the Fast Lane

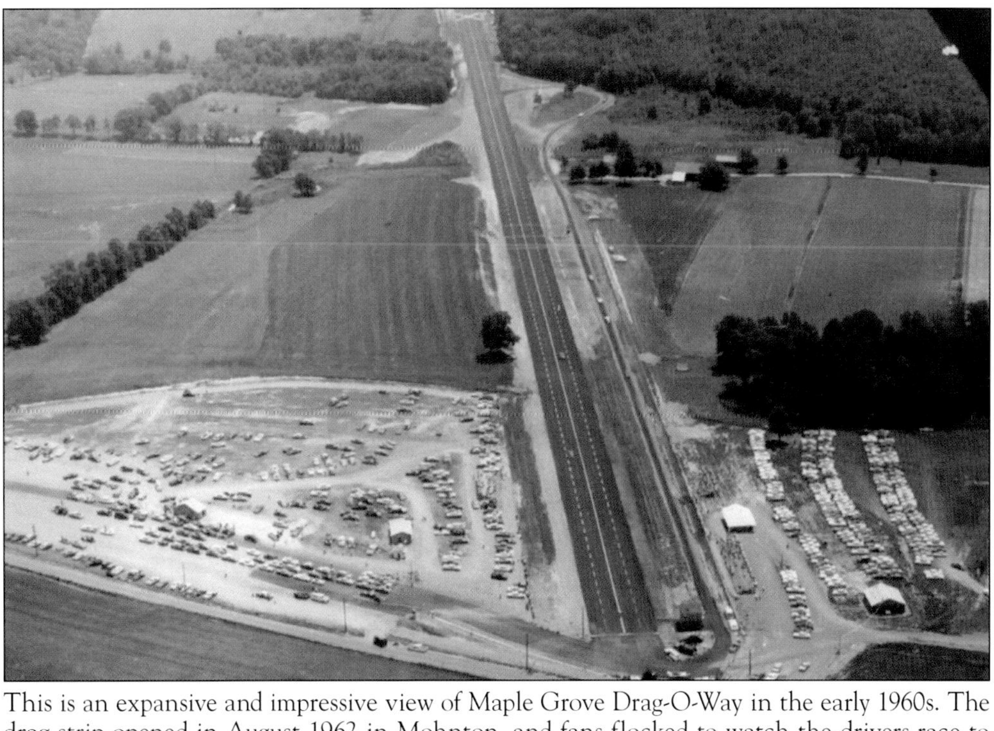

This is an expansive and impressive view of Maple Grove Drag-O-Way in the early 1960s. The drag strip opened in August 1962 in Mohnton, and fans flocked to watch the drivers race to the finish line. Drivers enjoyed racing, signing autographs, and making memories together. A park and pool brought many people from around the state to camp out throughout the summer. (Courtesy of Maple Grove Raceway.)

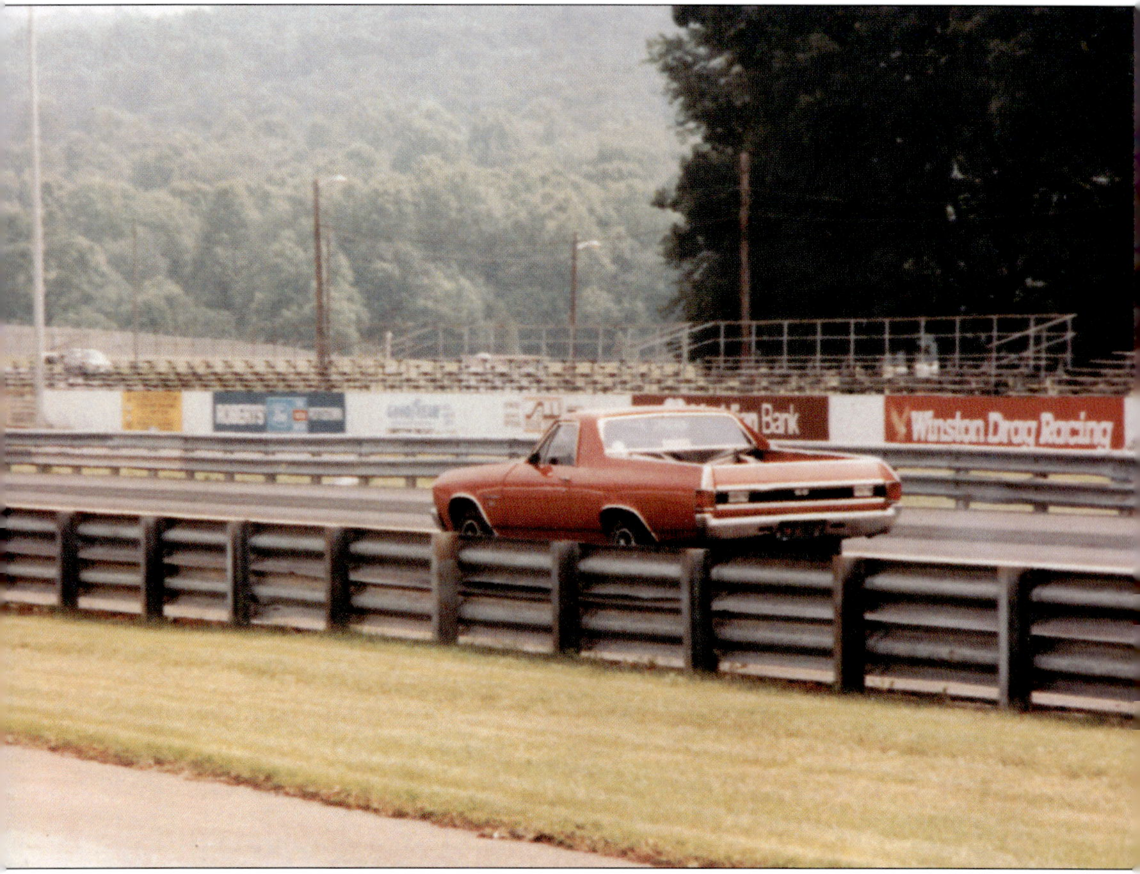

John Puccella of Pottstown makes a pass at Maple Grove Raceway in the late 1980s. He made about a dozen passes on the track and also enjoyed being a spectator. Pucella was an avid cruiser in Pottstown in the 1980s through the early 1990s. It helped him gain a lot of knowledge about cars while he also enjoyed hanging out with his friends and taking photographs of the cruisers enjoying their hobby. (Courtesy of John Puccella.)

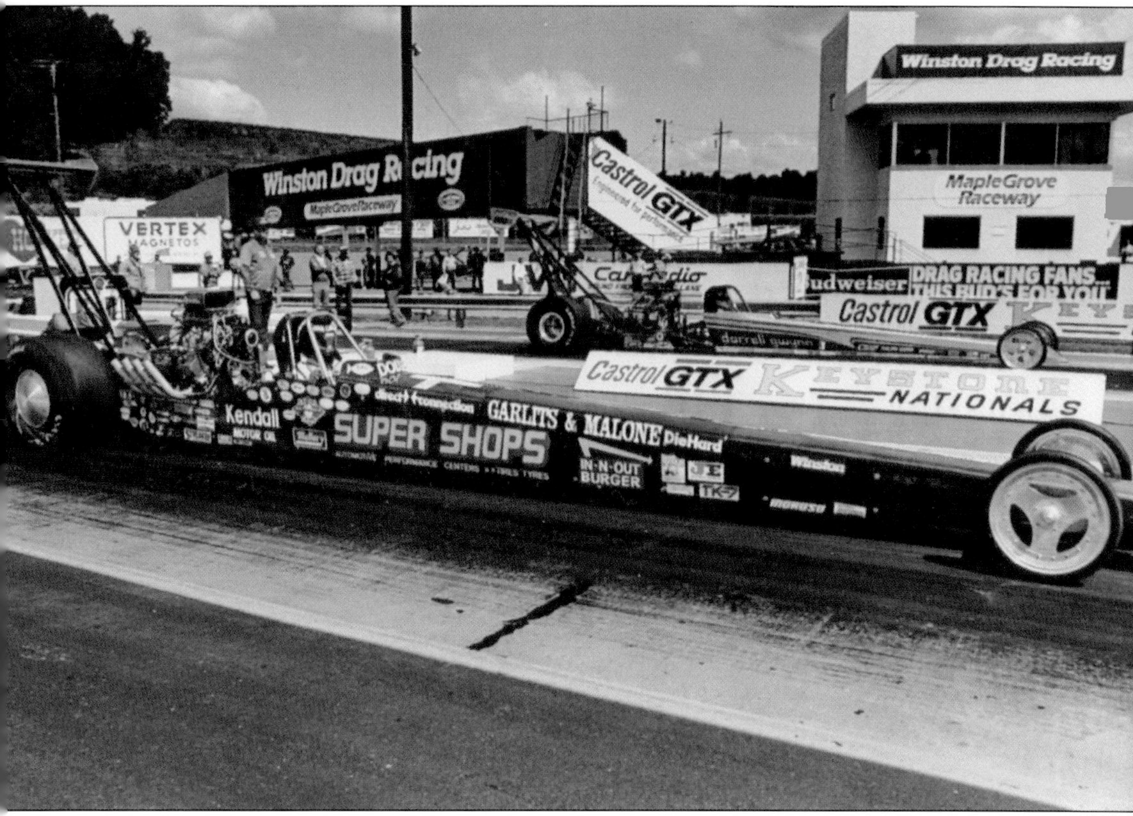

"Big Daddy" Don Garlits (foreground) takes on Darell Gwynn at Maple Grove Raceway in the 1970s. Both drivers played a major part in racing at "the Grove" over the many years of their careers. Each driver had incredible wins, which led to them being added to the Walk of Fame. They are well known in the National Hot Rod Association (NHRA) as Top Fuelers and for their many contributions to the sport. (Courtesy of Maple Grove Raceway.)

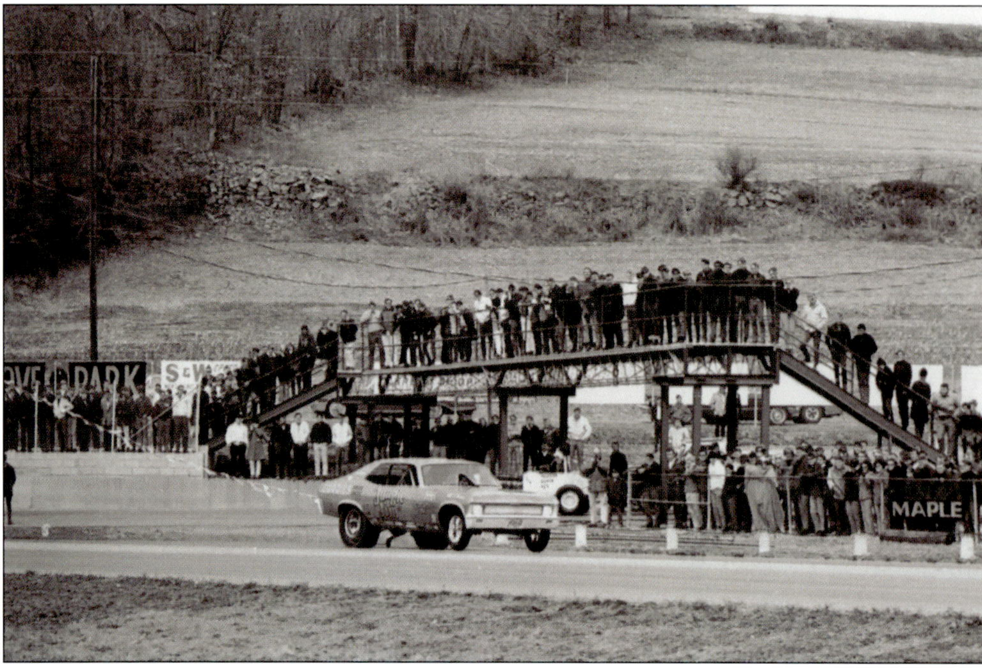

"Jungle Jim" Liberman of West Chester was one of the most popular drag racers to compete at Maple Grove Raceway. Liberman was famous across the country and won countless drag races before his life was cut short during an accident on the highway. He is shown here at the starting line while fans and photographers watch for his next move. (Courtesy of Maple Grove Raceway.)

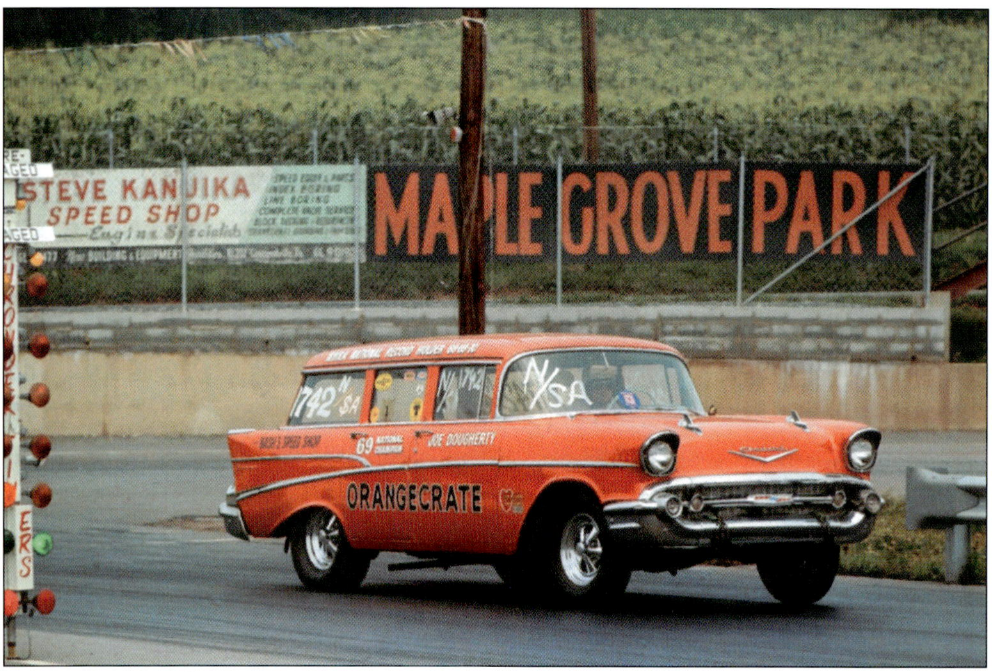

In 1970, Joe Dougherty drives his Orange Crate wagon. Many drivers had names for their cars; this made it easier to remind fans of their favorites. Some drivers drove different cars throughout their careers, and most drivers raced at several tracks, too. (Courtesy of Maple Grove Raceway.)

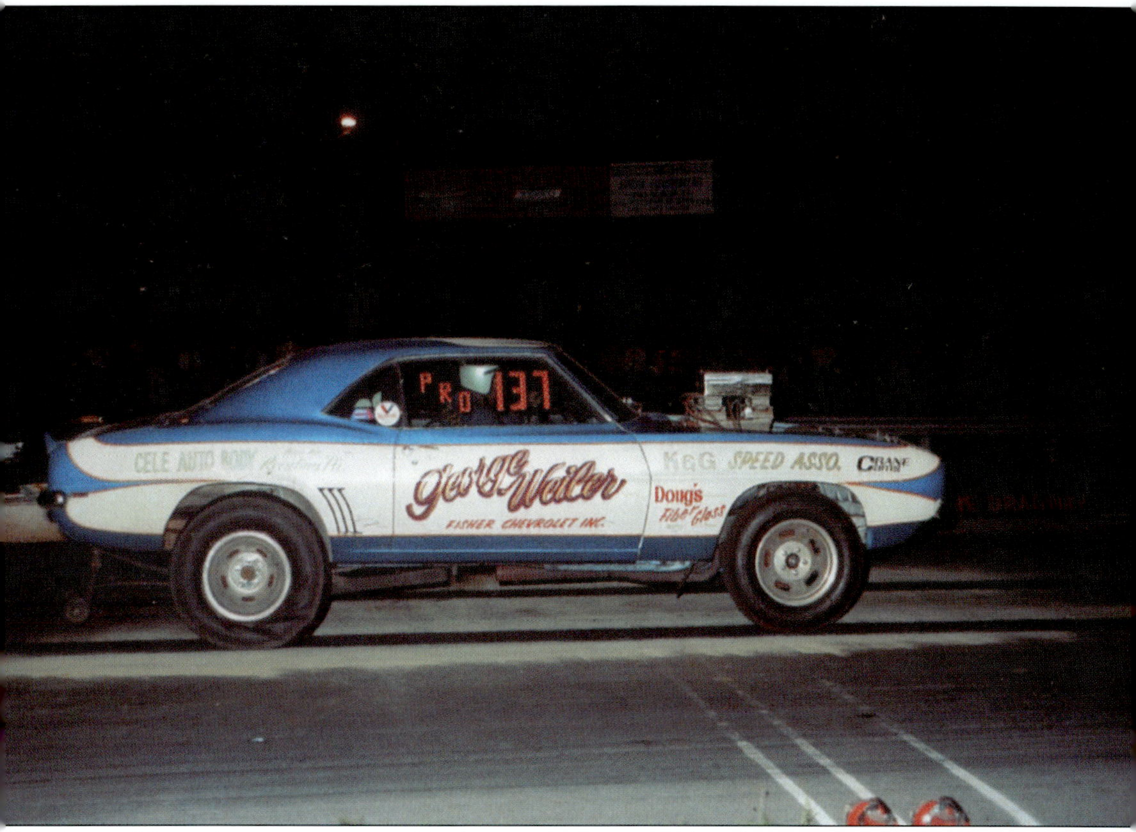

George Weiter, shown here racing at Maple Grove Raceway, was largely responsible for the existence of Maple Grove Raceway. In 1962, he convinced landowner Alfred Stauffer to build the drag strip on his property. Along with Lee Crupi, Carl Ruth and Bob Eveland suggested converting the track so it could be a full-size drag strip. (Courtesy of Maple Grove Raceway.)

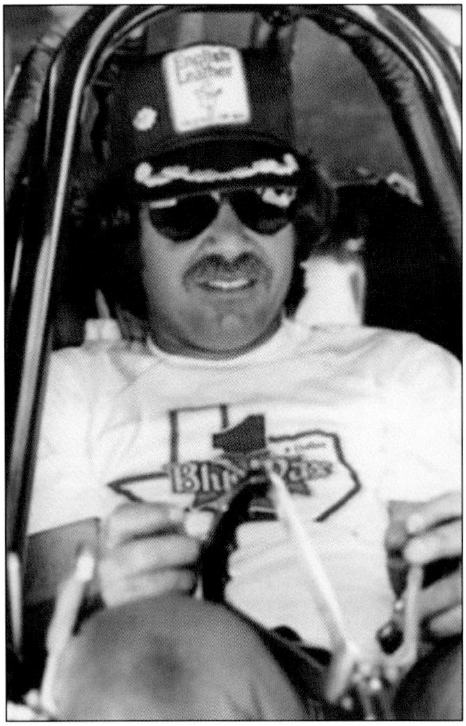

The late Ray Beadle was a drag racer and owner of the "Blue Max" funny car. He was named No. 20 of the National Hot Rod Association's greatest drivers in its first 50 years. Beadle was well known at Maple Grove Raceway and elsewhere for his fantastic track history and caring personality. (Courtesy of Maple Grove Raceway.)

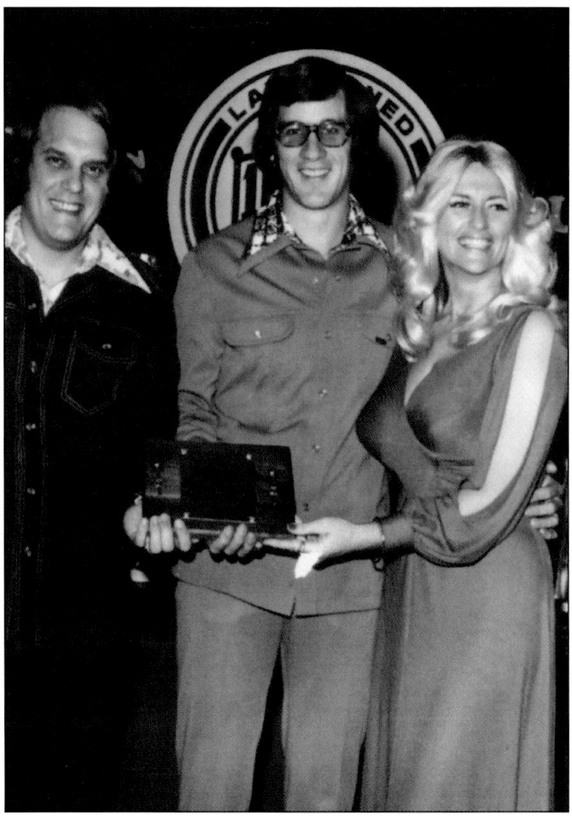

Maple Grove Raceway general manger Lex Dudas (left), general manager Mike Lewis (center), and Linda Vaughn ("Miss Hurst Golden Shifter") are pictured here. The 1970s were full of fun and fantastic races. Miss Golden Hurst Shifter first graced Maple Grove Raceway throughout the 1960s and still does today. She is legendary for her great poise and sexy look. Vaughn also earned her Sport Car Club of America (SCCA) license at the Bob Bondurant School of High Performance Driving and raced with passion. (Courtesy of Fred Spiezio.)

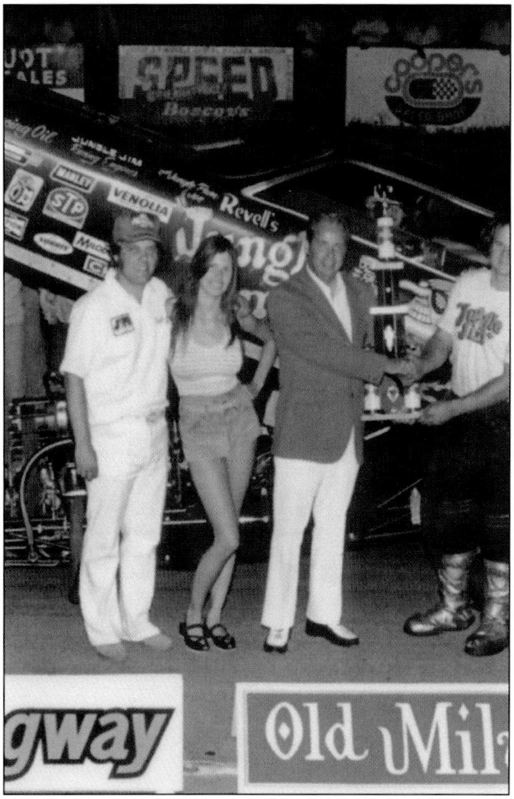

"Jungle Jim" Liberman receives a trophy on Winners Night at Maple Grove Raceway in the 1970s. He stands with Lex Dudas and "Jungle Pam" Hardy. He collected many trophies over his years in racing. "Jungle Jim" and "Jungle Pam" were known to put on a good show at every track, making them drag racing legends. (Courtesy of Maple Grove Raceway.)

Pictured here are, from left to right, Linda Vaughn ("Miss Hurst Golden Shifter"), Bill "Grumpy" Jenkins, Bebop Hobel ("Miss Winston"), and Lex Dudas. Dudas was the general manager of Maple Grove Raceway. They are enjoying a day at the track in the 1970s. (Courtesy of Fred Spiezio.)

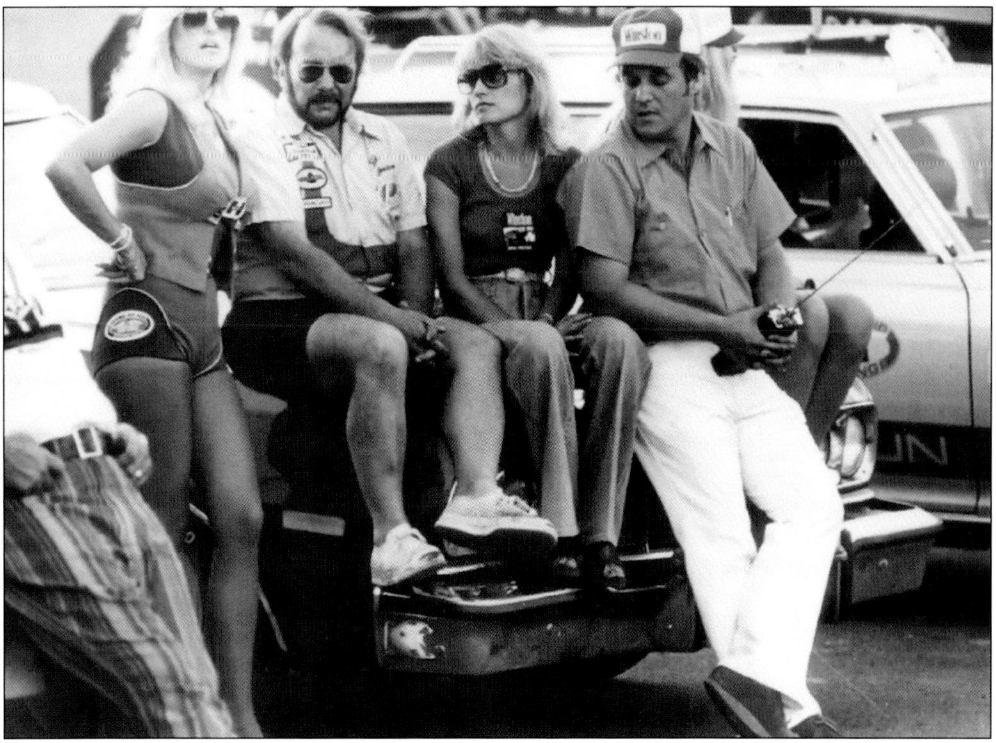

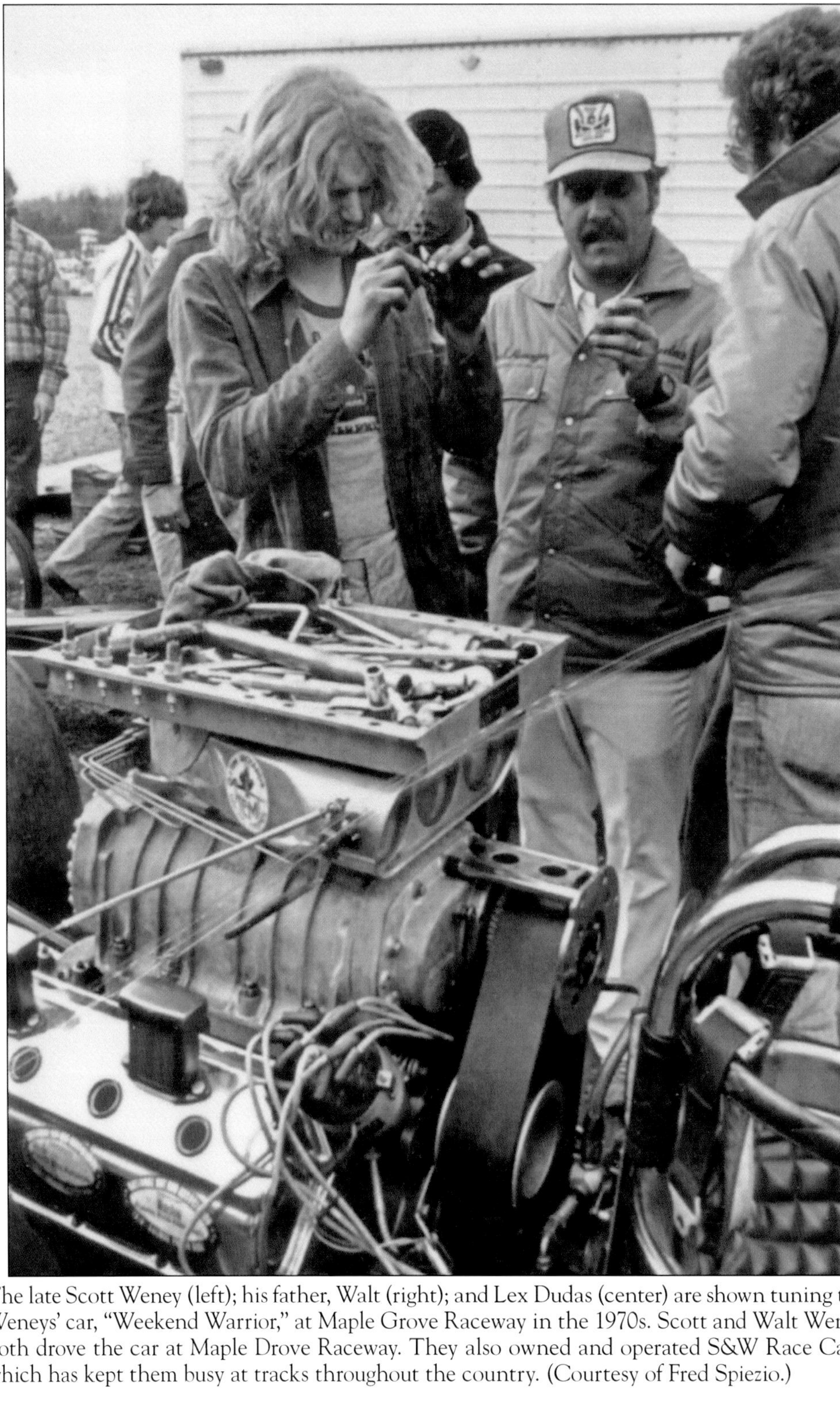

The late Scott Weney (left); his father, Walt (right); and Lex Dudas (center) are shown tuning the Weneys' car, "Weekend Warrior," at Maple Grove Raceway in the 1970s. Scott and Walt Weney both drove the car at Maple Drove Raceway. They also owned and operated S&W Race Cars, which has kept them busy at tracks throughout the country. (Courtesy of Fred Spiezio.)

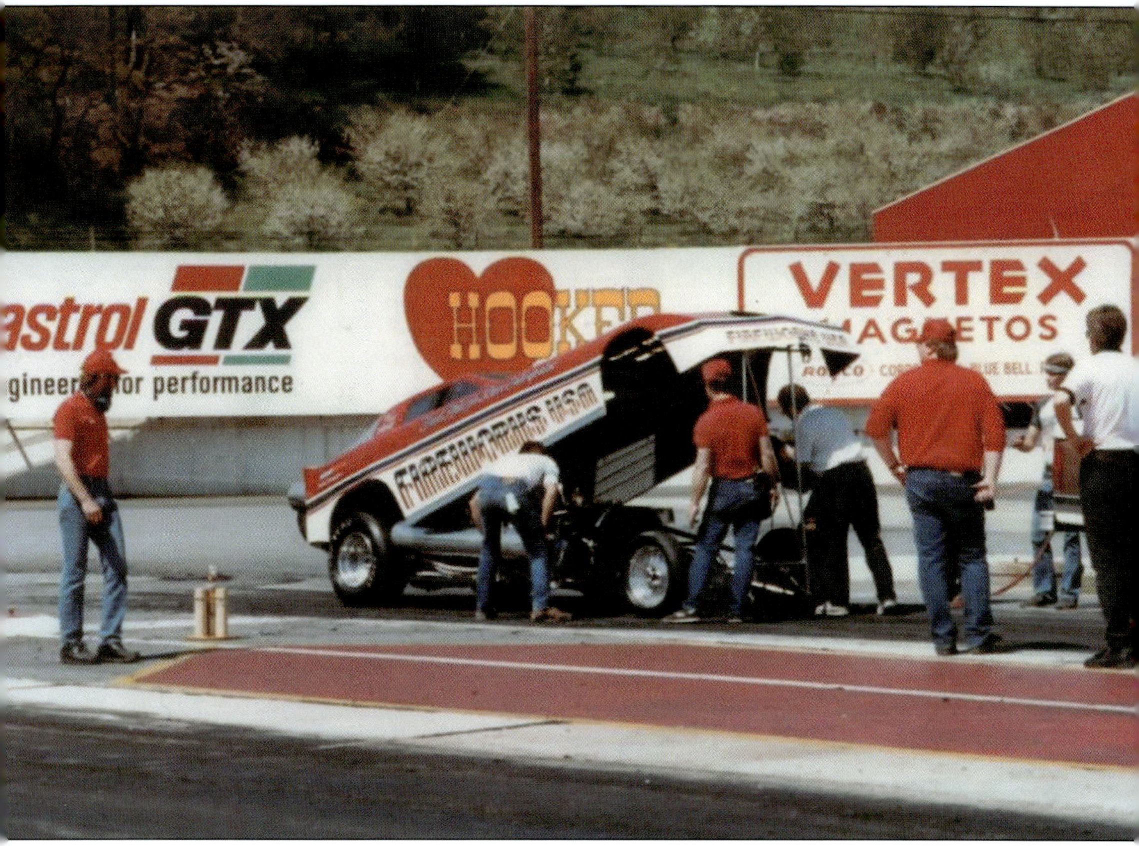

Fred Spiezio's "Fireworks USA" jet funny car was built in 1984 on Charlotte Street by Meng Racing Specialties. It has a J-34-34 with Bunssci jet fighter engine. Scott Shaffer drove the car at Maple Grove Raceway and other tracks. It was also taken to Arizona and Texas, then driven for four more years in Pennsylvania. (Courtesy of Fred Spiezio.)

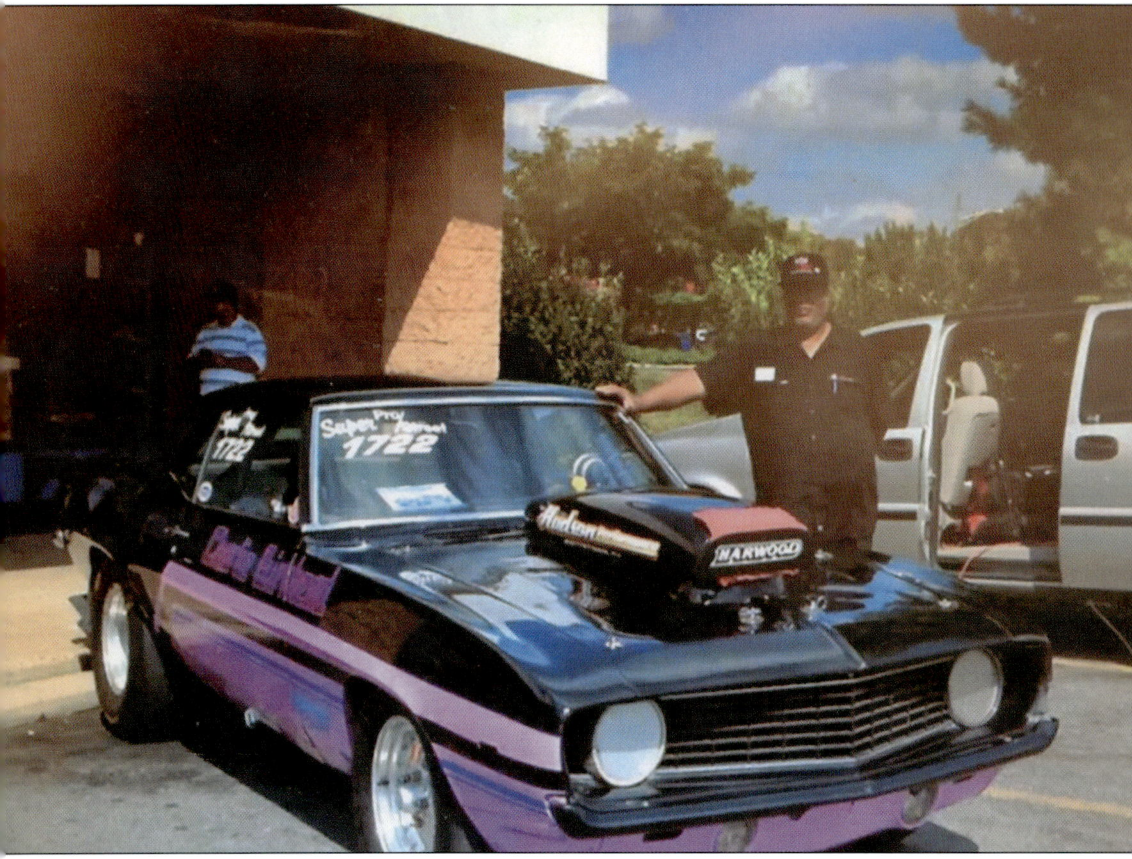

Charlie Birckhead Sr. has been racing at Maple Grove Raceway since the late 1960s and continues to race today. He races a Super Pro Street 1722 Camaro drag car, which he enjoys racing at Englishtown, Atco, New Media, and surrounding local tracks. Charlie Sr. has continued the tradition of racing with his wife, Linda Birckhead, who has been racing for seven years, and his son, Charlie Birckhead Jr., who has been racing for five years. Charlie Sr. is also the manager at Pep Boys in Reading. He holds a car show each year and hosts the Cars and Coffee event each month at this location. (Courtesy of Charlie Birckhead Sr.)

Lex Dudas (right) presents the award for sponsor of the year to Jack Duffy of Hurst Performance, Inc., in 1975. Sponsorship has always been important for drivers and a track to succeed. It can increase business and help cover financial expenses. Occasionally, a driver will not have sponsorship, but this is rare. (Courtesy of Fred Spiezio.)

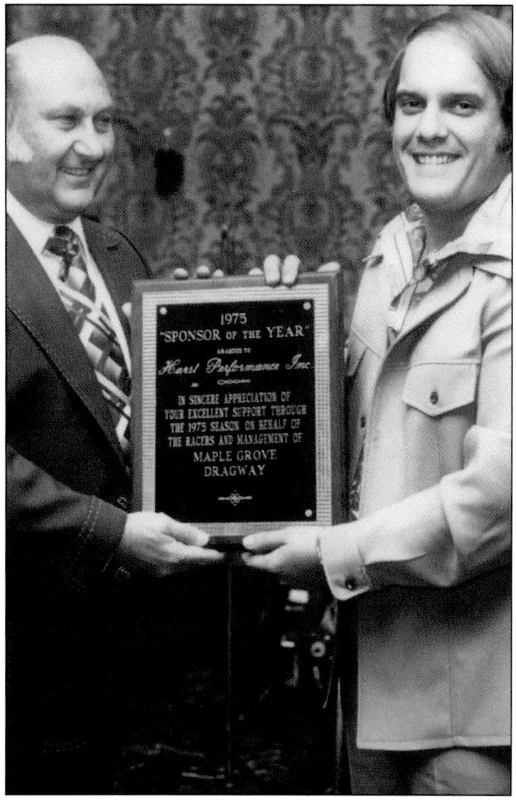

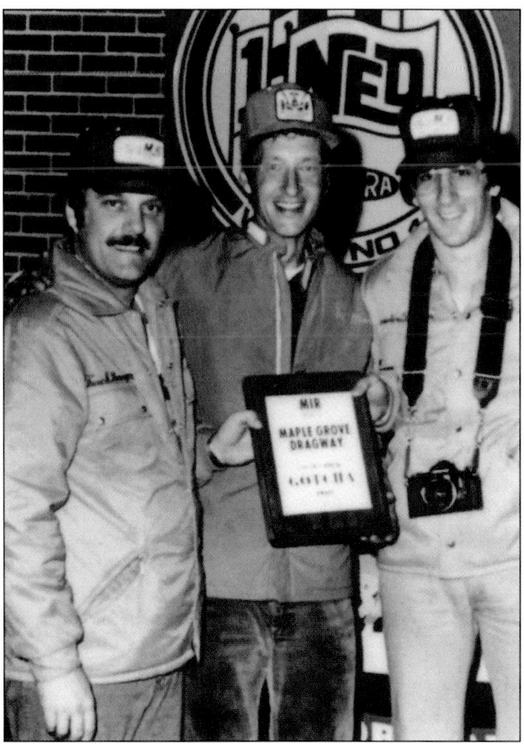

Maple Grove Raceway is a very popular racetrack. Well known throughout Montgomery and Berks Counties and across the country, it has won awards for its many contributions to the sport of racing. In 1974, the National Hot Rod Association named it Division 1 Track of the Year—an award the track won several more times. (Courtesy of Maple Grove Raceway.)

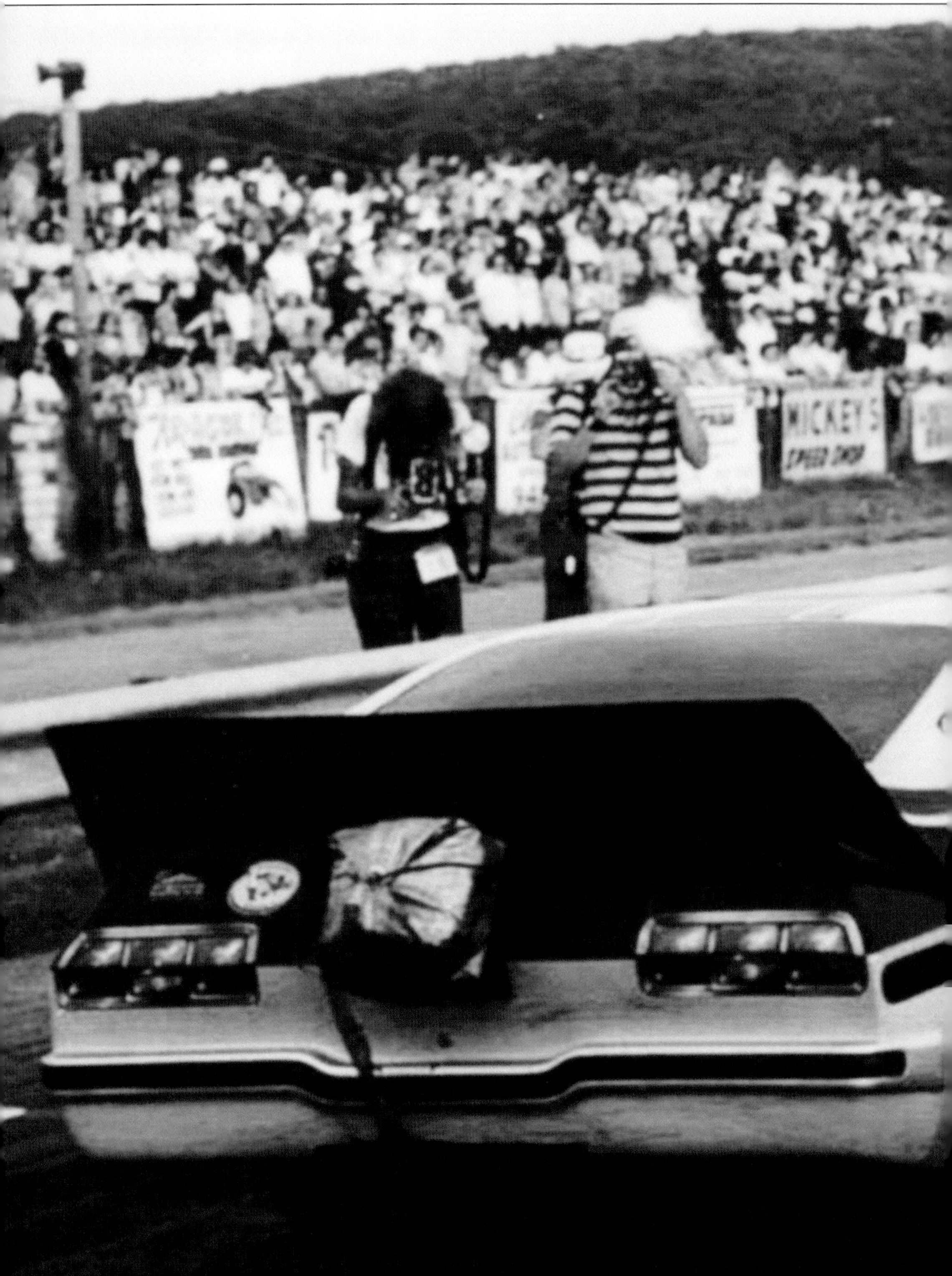
MICKEY'S
SPEED SHOP

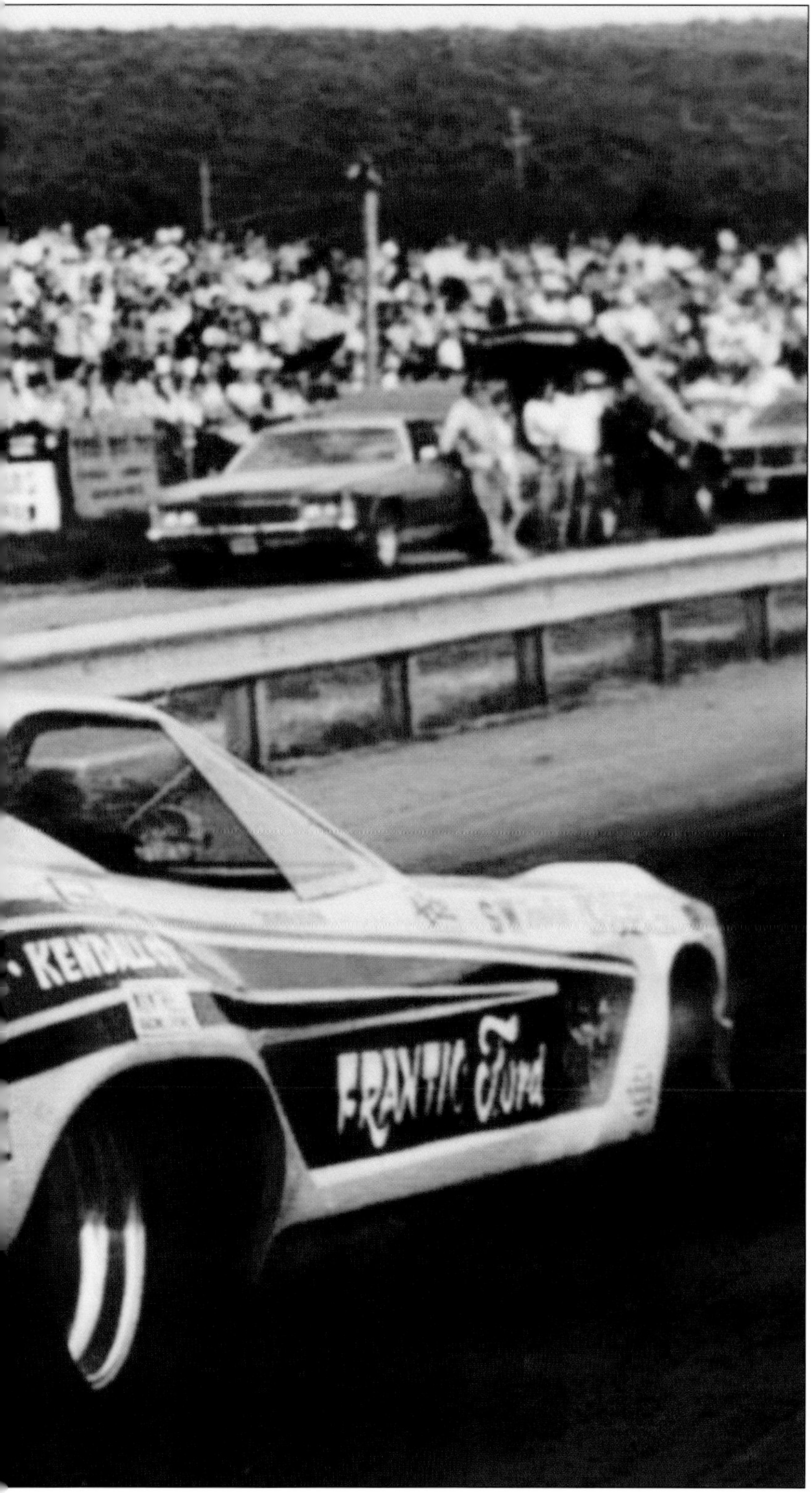

The late Paul "Dodger" Glenn is shown here in 1975 at Maple Grove Raceway. Prior to driving the Frantic Ford AA/FC, Dodger spent time handling the driving chores in a few East Coast–based top-fuel machines before switching to funny cars. So beloved by fans for his great driving abilities and positive attitude, Glenn was a wonderful man who shared his love of racing not only with his fans and coworkers, but also with his family. He was a true legend and will forever be loved. (Courtesy of Jim Cutler.)

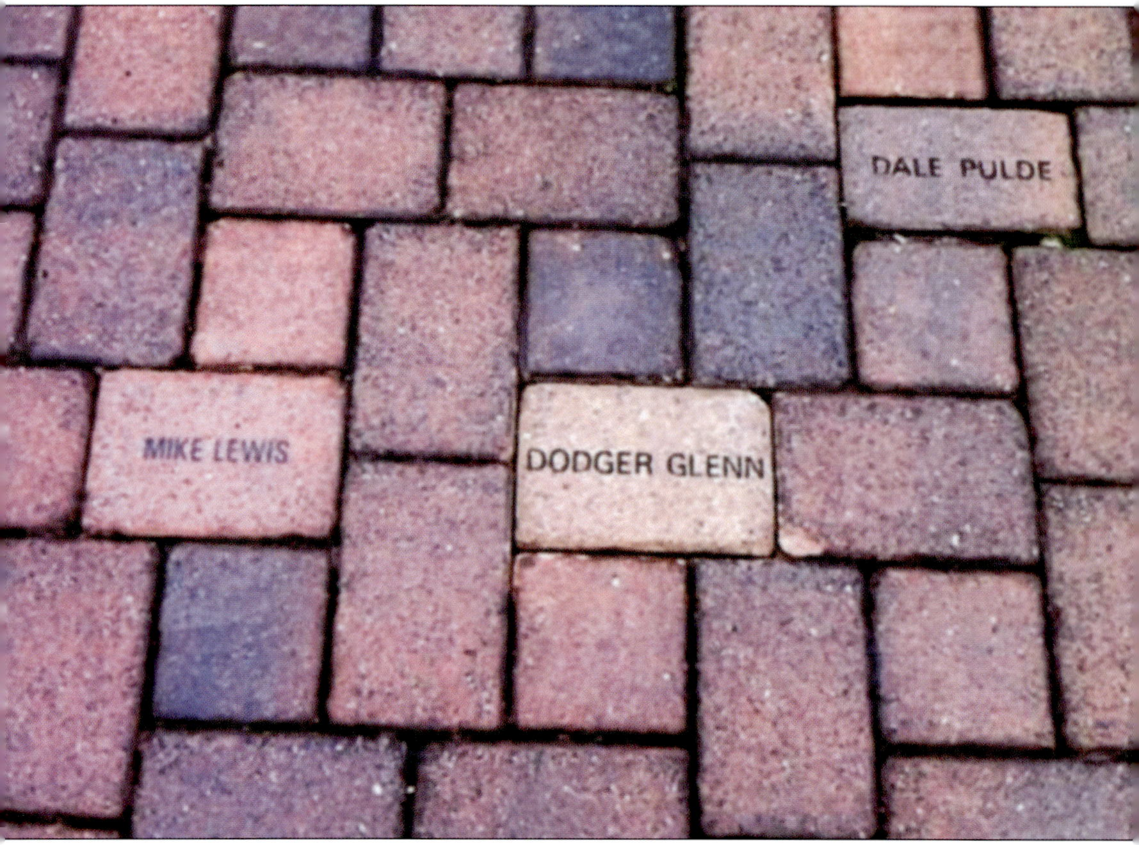

In 2012, Dodger Glenn, Dale Pulde, Raymond Beadle, Don Prudhomme, and Frank Hawley were inducted into the Walk of Fame. The first class was inducted in 2003; 78 participants have been inducted to date. Each inductee has made Maple Grove Raceway a great place to watch one of today's favorite sports. (Courtesy of Bobby Frey.)

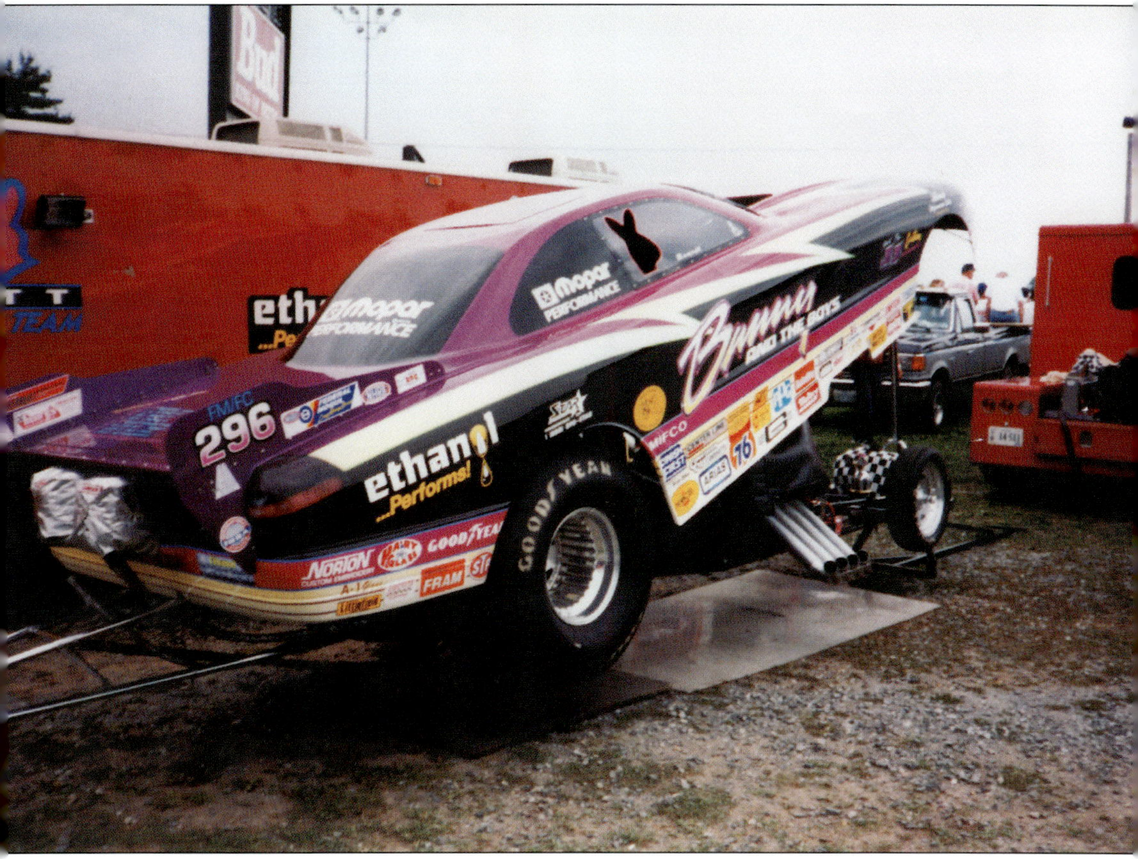

Bunny Burkett displays her jet car, "Bunny and the Boys," at Maple Grove Raceway. She has been a legend in funny car racing for over 50 years. During her time in racing, Bunny was a National Hot Rod Association champion, inducted in the East Coast Drag Times Hall of Fame, and enjoyed many more great accomplishments. She has a large and passionate group of fans and a wonderful crew. (Courtesy of Mike Strouse.)

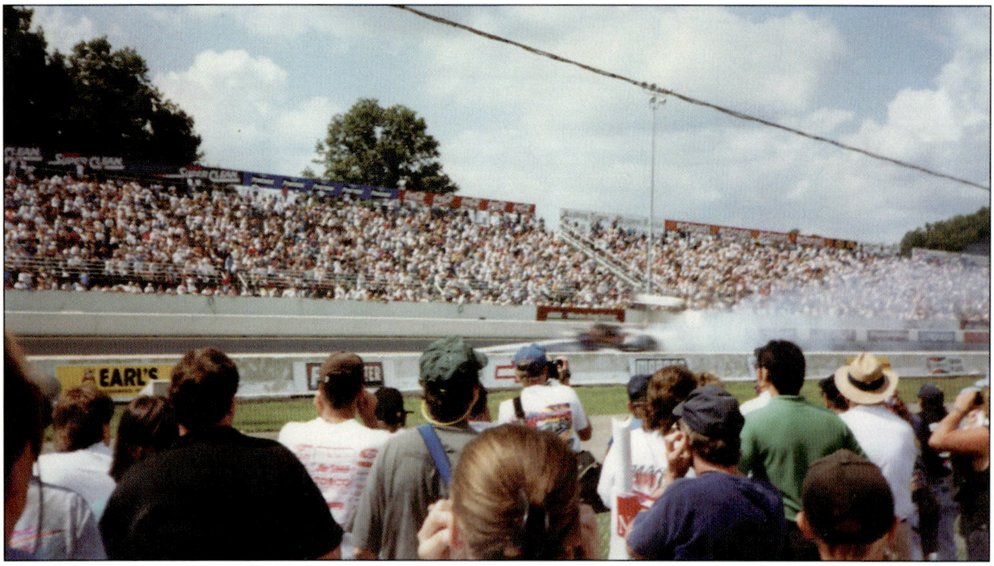

Crowds fill the stands at Maple Grove Raceway each season. Each year brings thousands of fans who come to see their favorites and newcomers. The track has changed much over the years, including the addition of new grandstands with reserved seating, a VIP hospitality tower, and a track lighting system. The beautiful sky shown here allows for another great day of racing, giving families and friends a place to make wonderful memories. (Courtesy of Mike Strouse.)

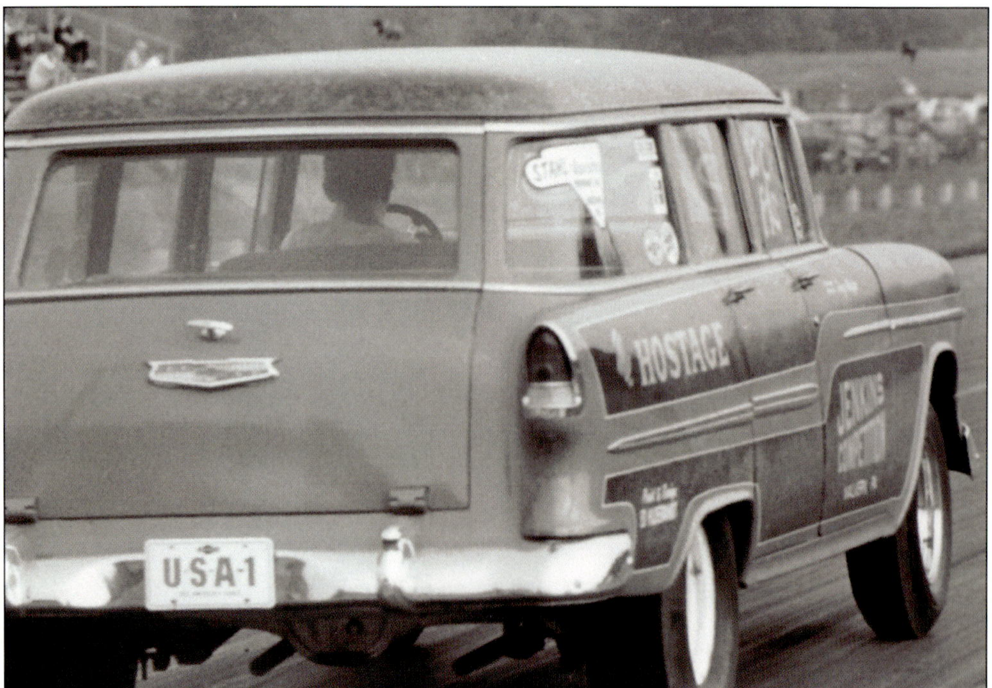

Doug Mentzer drove his car, "Hostage," at Maple Grove Raceway and other tracks. Mentzer won 13 national records with a Jenkins Competition engine. In 1970, he won the Junior Stock Eliminator, which took place on Saturday nights. He always enjoyed racing and having a good time. (Courtesy of Carl Rubright.)

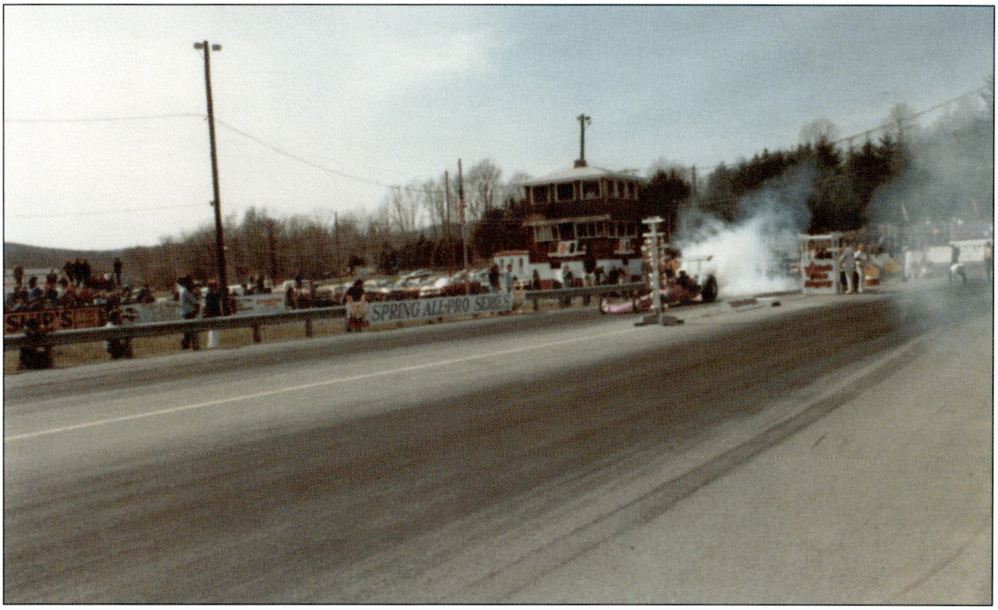

Shirley Muldowney, known as the "First Lady of Drag Racing," has shown her courage, strength, and love of competition at Maple Grove Raceway and racetracks across the country. In 1965, Muldowney was the first woman to receive her license to drive a dragster. She won the National Hot Rod Association (NHRA) Top Fuel championship in 1977, 1980, and 1982, making her the first person to win two (and then three) Top Fuel titles. Muldowney won 18 NHRA national events, which encouraged women to try the sport. She raced against many other great drivers, such as Don Garlits, Conrad "Connie" Kalitta, and Tommy Ivo, making her a fan favorite. Muldowney will be making appearances at races throughout 2016. (Both, courtesy of Fred Spiezio.)

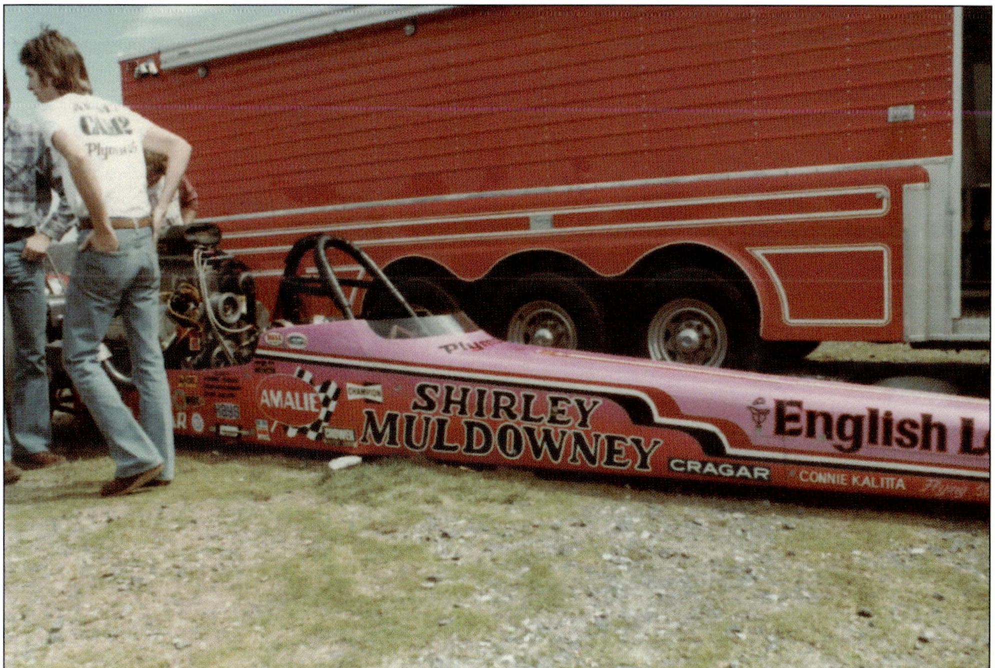

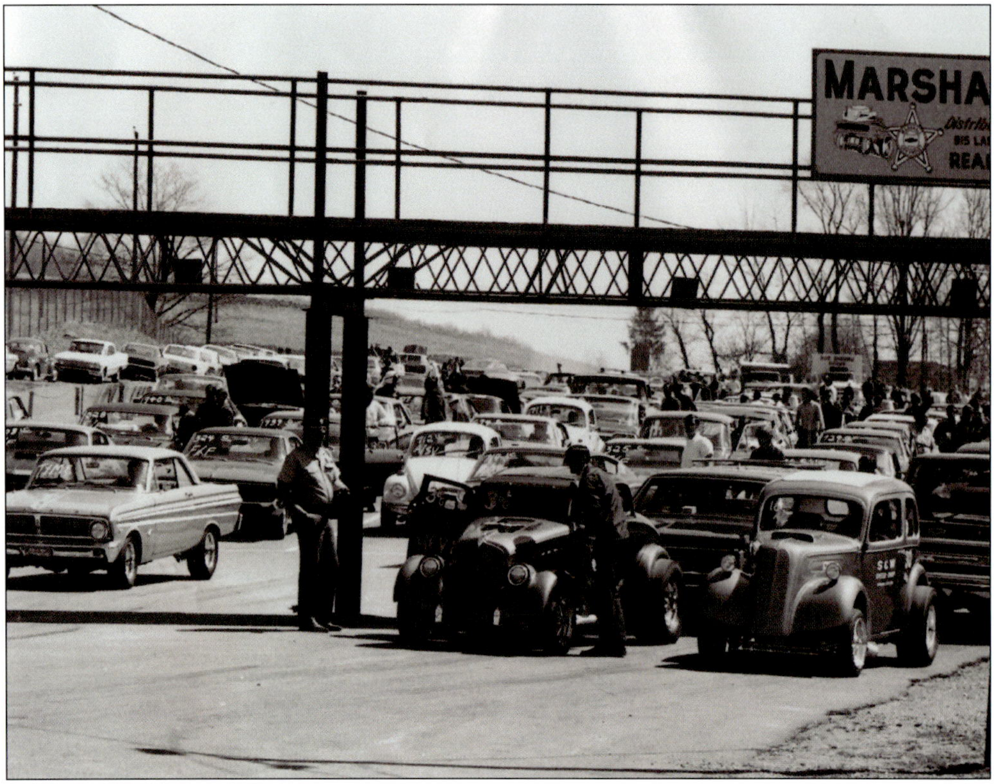

Cars line up at the starting line at Maple Grove Raceway in the early 1970s. The starting line began after a sharp left turn. It was quite an experience to spend time at the track, making for a day of fun and excitement. Each driver waited with anticipation for those moments spent racing down the track. (Courtesy of Carl Rubrecht.)

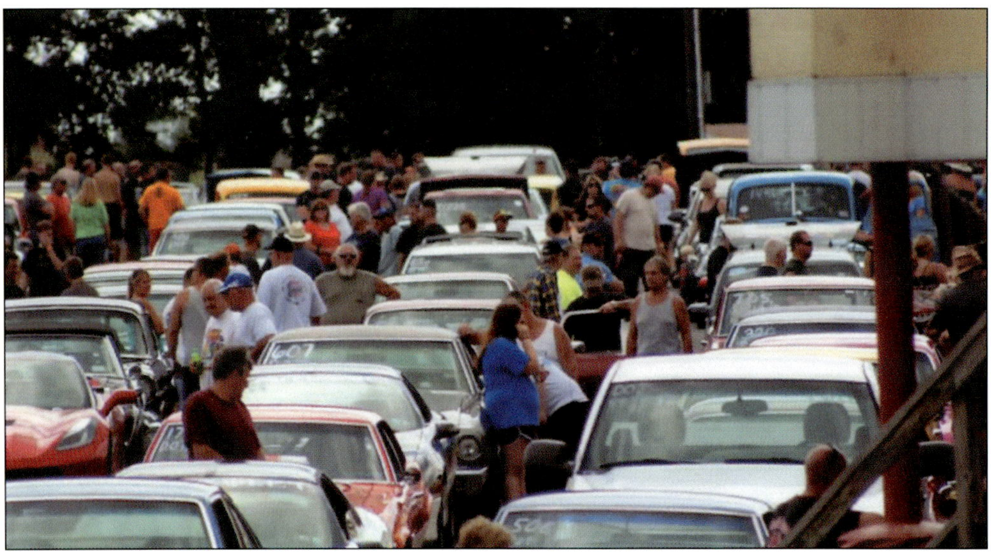

The staging lane is always an interesting place full of excited participants. Each driver is hoping for a win at Maple Grove Raceway. This race was held during the Super Chevy event in July 2015. It cost participants between $15 and $100 to race. (Courtesy of Bill Salter.)

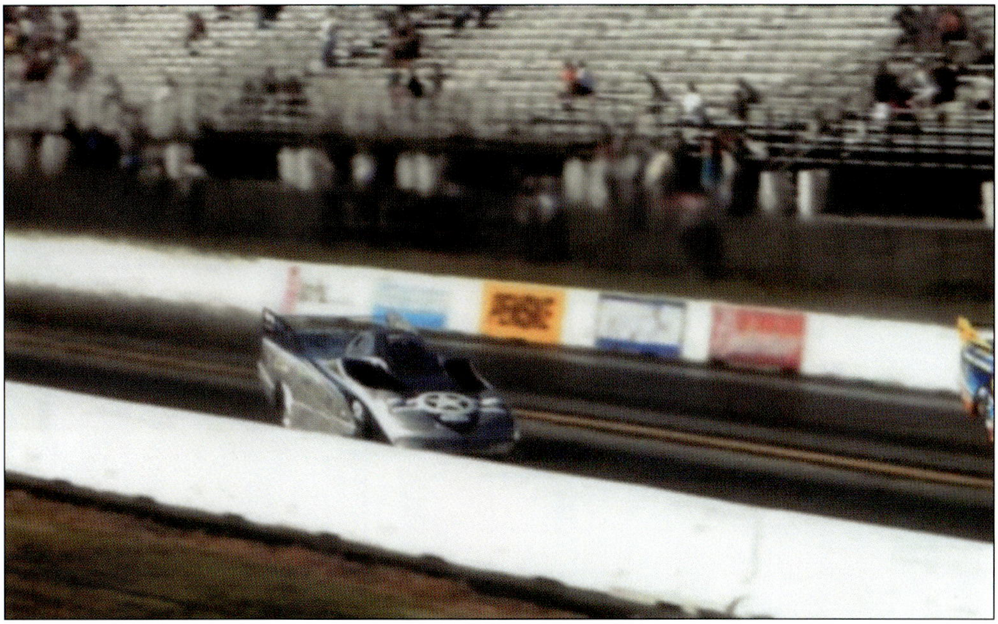

Ken Hall, pictured here at Maple Grove Raceway, travels the United States, Canada, and Puerto Rico for appearances. Hall is the driver for Hanna Motorsports, and he drives the Xlerator jet funny car, which is known to be the highest-tech jet funny car in history. He grew up at Maple Grove Raceway with his legendary father, Harry Hall. Ken also races against his brother Mike Hall, and the two are often spotted together at car shows in Montgomery and Berks Counties, often surrounded by tons of fans wanting to take pictures and get autographs. Tori Hall, Mike's daughter, is now winning her own trophies in junior dragster competitions. (Both, courtesy of Ken Hall.)

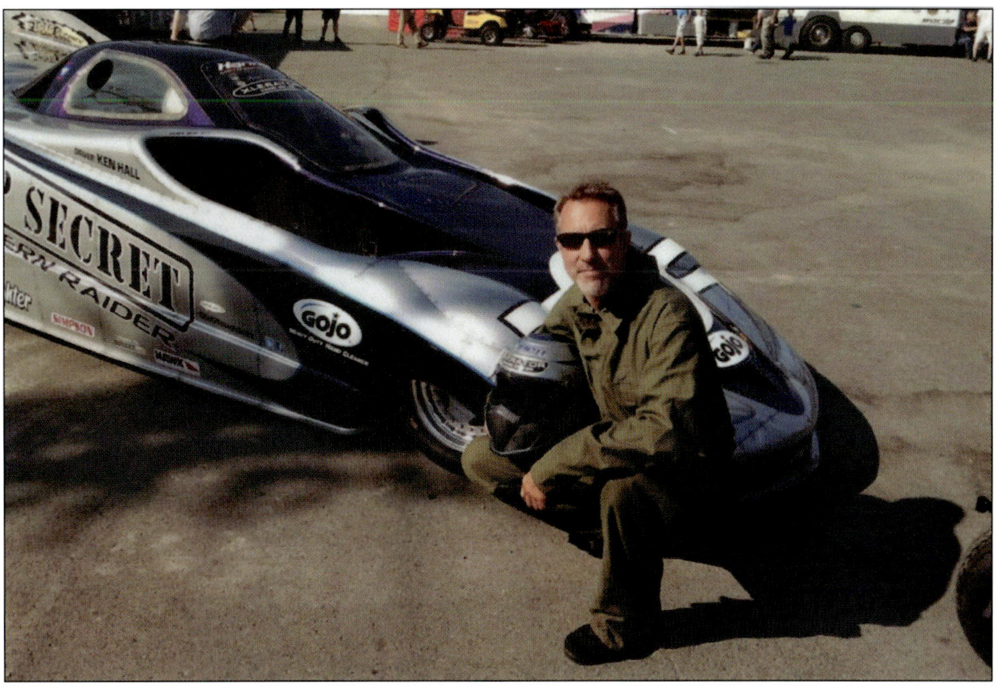

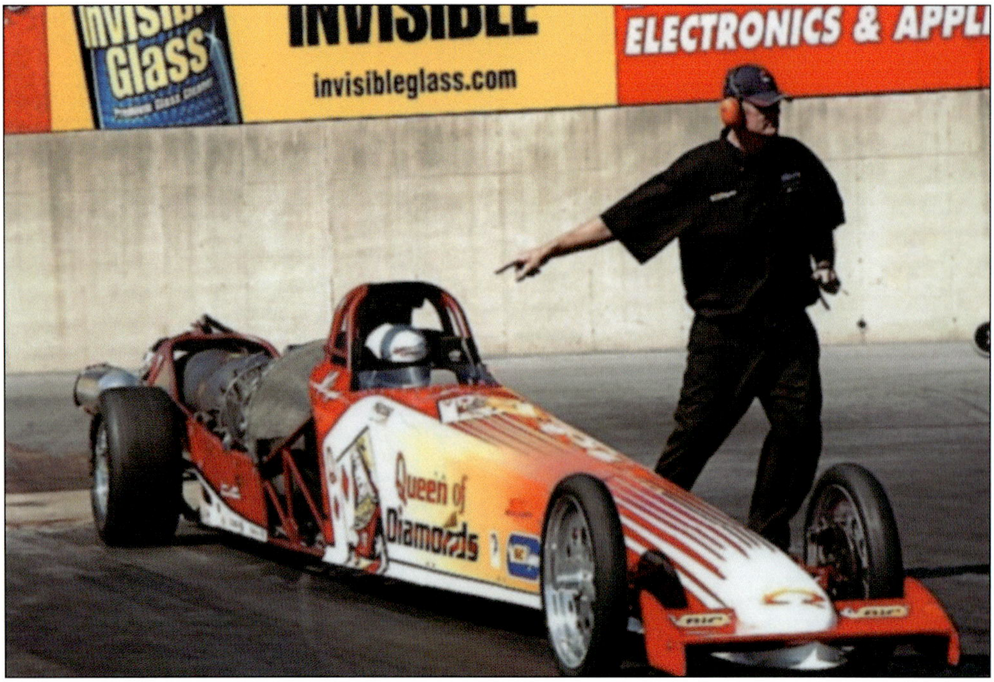

Jill Canuso Fazekas drives a jet car called "Queen of Diamonds" and owned by Hanna Sports Pro Race. She was the first nitro funny car driver to go 200 mph at Maple Grove Raceway. Fazekas is also the marketing director at S&W Race Cars in Spring City, Pennsylvania. Al Hanna is shown here interacting with Fazekas. (Courtesy of Jill Canuso Fazekas.)

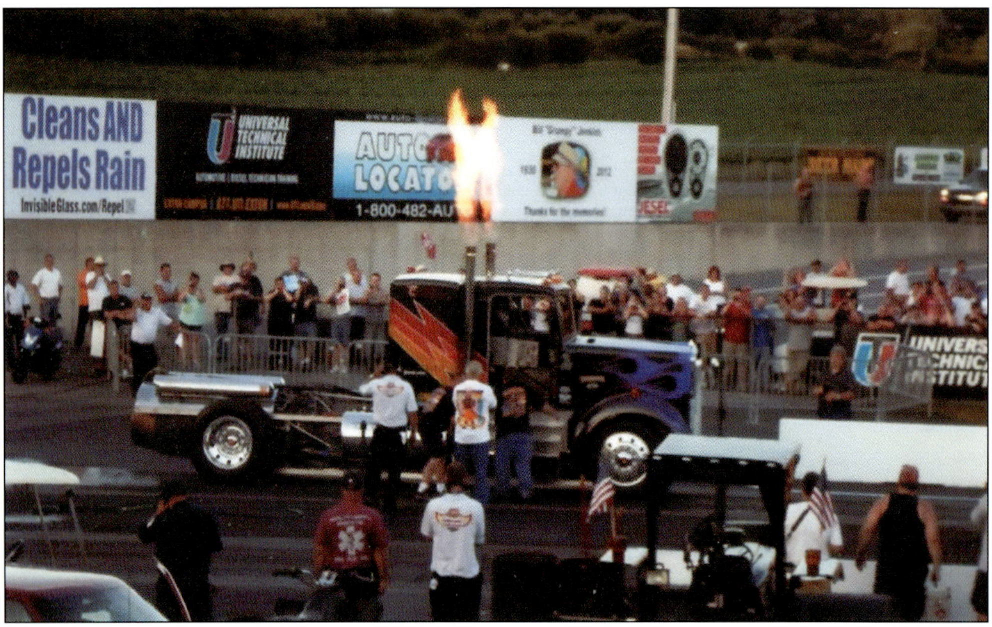

Bob Motz is shown here racing his original jet truck at Maple Grove Raceway's 50th anniversary celebration on June 23, 2012. Motz and his son Scott created this astonishing truck, a 1998 W900 Kenworth Continental Sleeper. The first jet truck to run over 200 mph in a quarter mile, it is incredible to watch. (Courtesy of George Zlumlord Watters.)

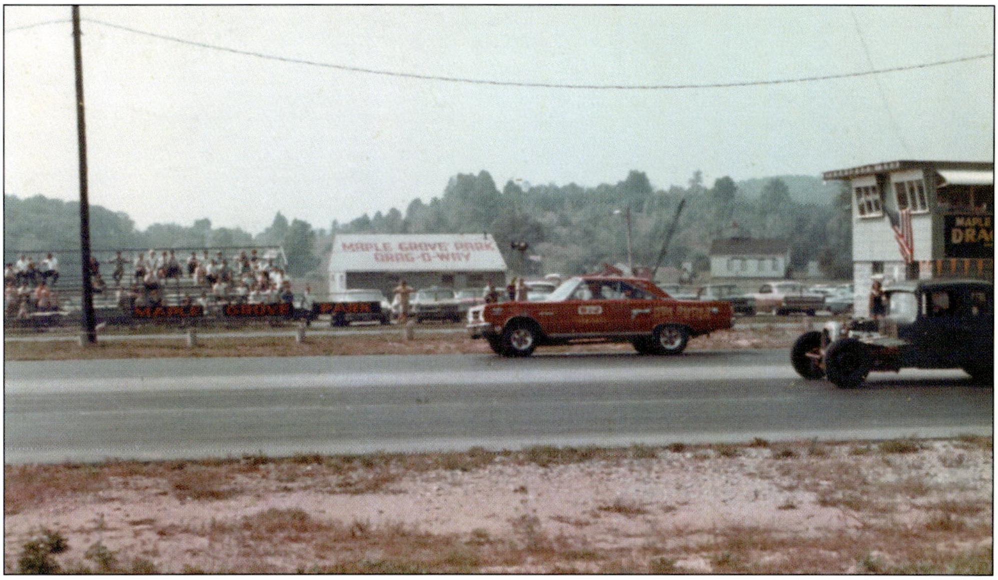

Joe Dillion drove his 1967 JTX 440 in Super Stock F Automatic at Maple Grove Raceway from 1967 to 1970. This gave Dillion over 100 wins to his name. He often raced at Atco Raceway, US 13 Dragway, Old Bridge Township Park (in Englishtown, New Jersey), Quakertown Speedway, and Cecil County Dragway. Maple Grove was considered his home track. (Courtesy of Joseph Dillion.)

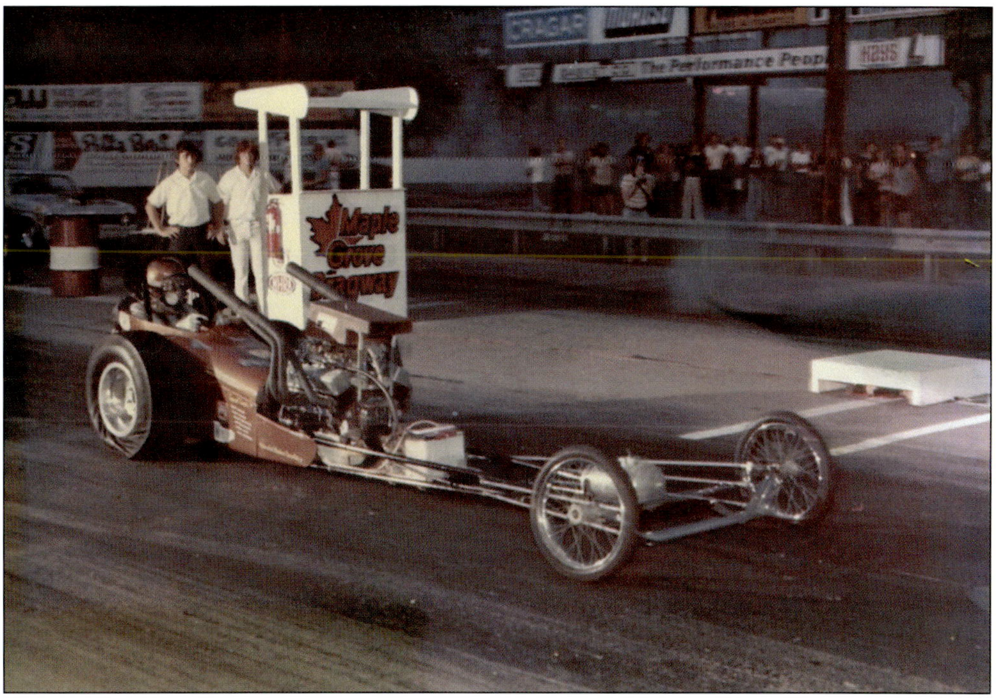

John Johnson is shown here racing in 1975 at Maple Grove Raceway. His first dragster, the Original Quarter Pounder, was purchased from Dave Grubb. He worked at Maple Grove Raceway as an announcer, in pit control, and at the starting line. Johnson passed his love of racing on to his son Kevin Johnson, who is now the owner of the New Quarter Pounder. They both work on their 1967 Camaro nostalgia funny car, "Glory Days." (Courtesy of John Johnson.)

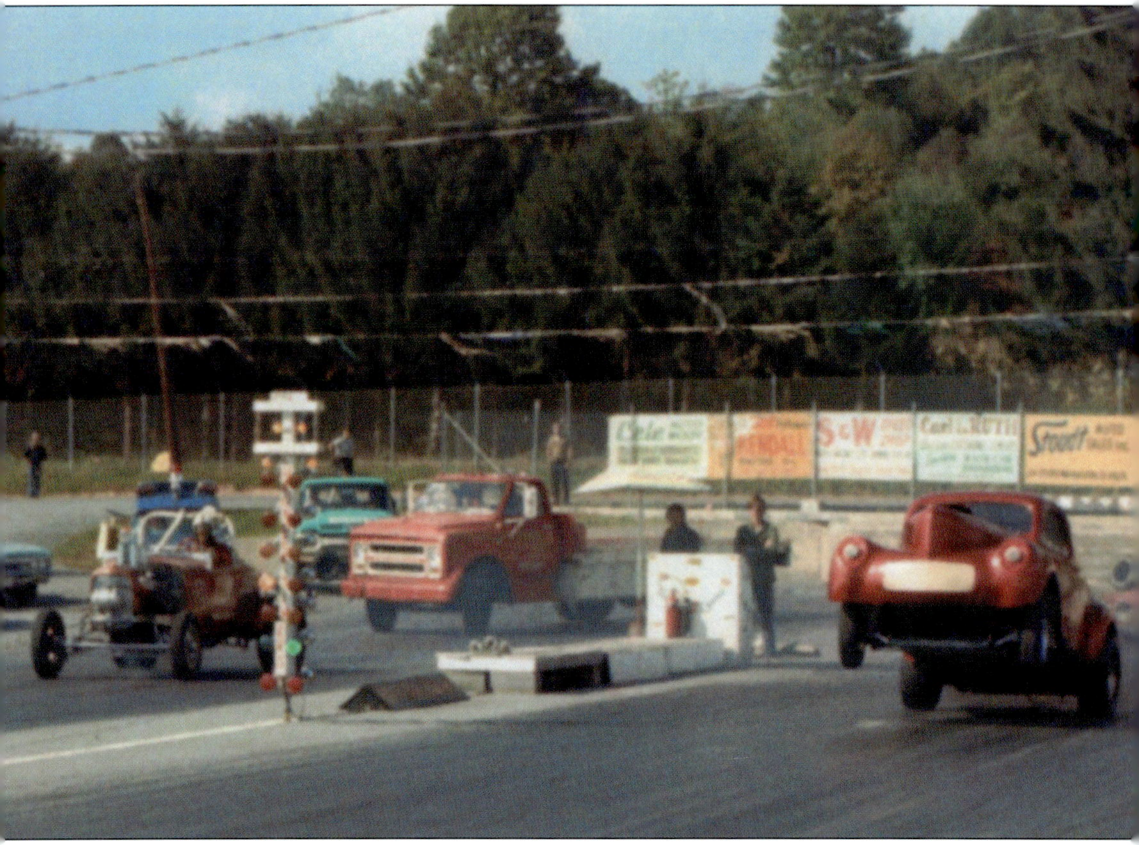

Anthony Ziemba and Carroll Hines are veteran Maple Grove Raceway drivers. Here, they are racing in the early 1970s. Ziemba is driving his Willys (right), and Hines is in his 1932 Roadster. Ziemba raced at Maple Grove from 1967 until 1993; his son Paul Ziemba also raced on several tracks in his 1973 Chevy Vega from 1979 to 1991. (Courtesy of Carl Rubrecht.)

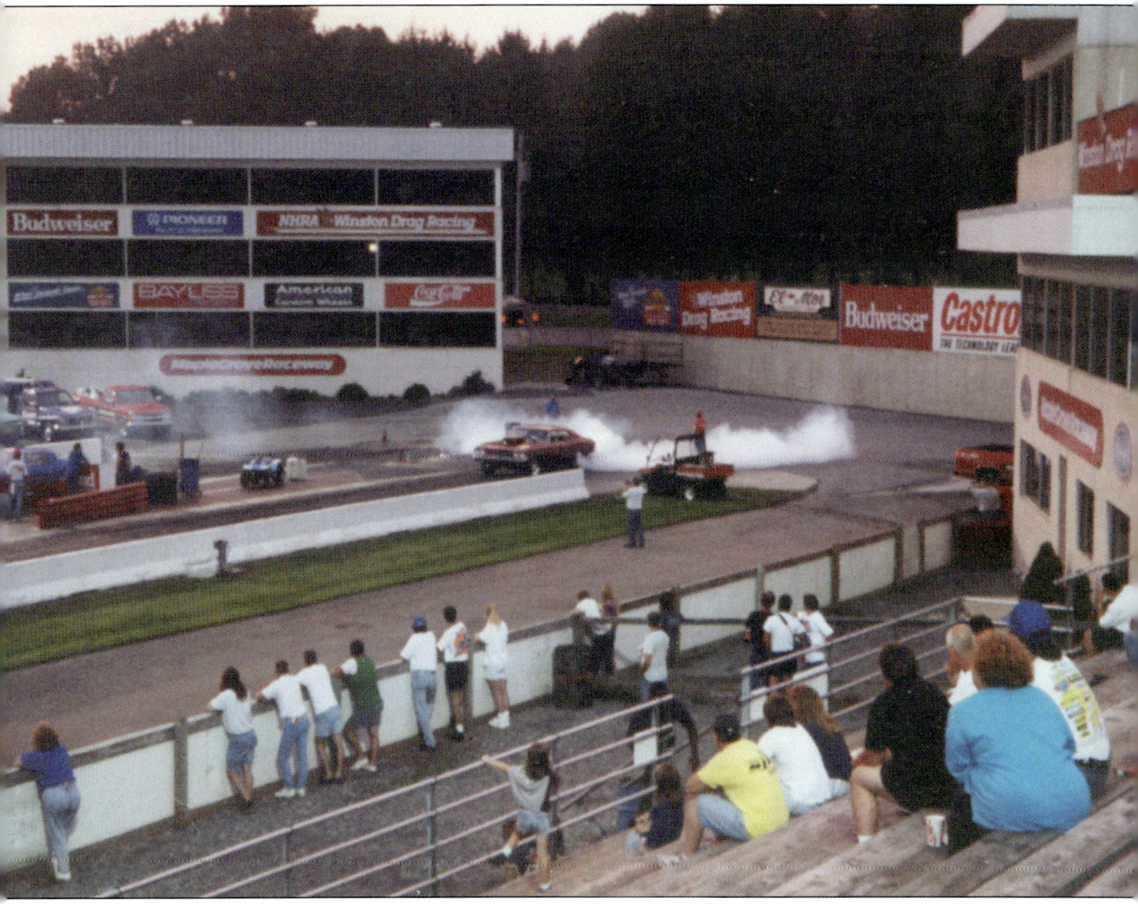

Mark Rubright, of Rubright Racing Enterprises, bought his first car—a 1968 Chevelle—in 1983. He wanted to make sure it was ready to drive when he turned 16, so he attended Western Montgomery Technical School and studied auto mechanics. He worked at Pep Boys and Midtown Tires in Pottstown while cruising on High Street with his brother Harold. In 1988, he started drag racing, in which he raced in the King of the Streets series. Later, in 1994, Rubright drove in the Fastest Street Car Shootout. In 2016, he will participate in grudge racing at Cecil County Dragway. (Courtesy of Mark Rubright.)

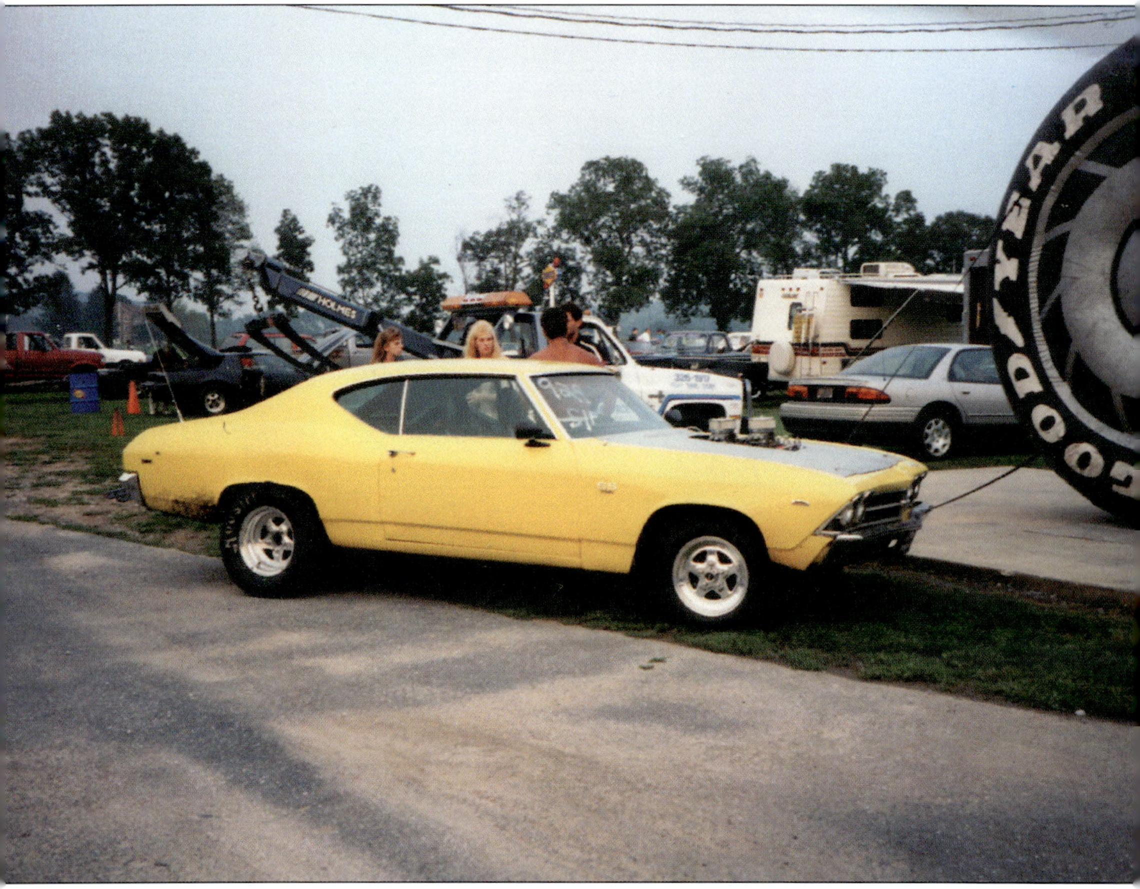

Anthony Navero is shown with his 1969 Chevelle Pro Street car at Maple Grove Raceway for a Friday night grudge match in 1993. He also raced on Route 422 in Montgomery and Berks Counties. Often, he would street race in Philadelphia with other drivers from the area. (Courtesy of Mark Rubright.)

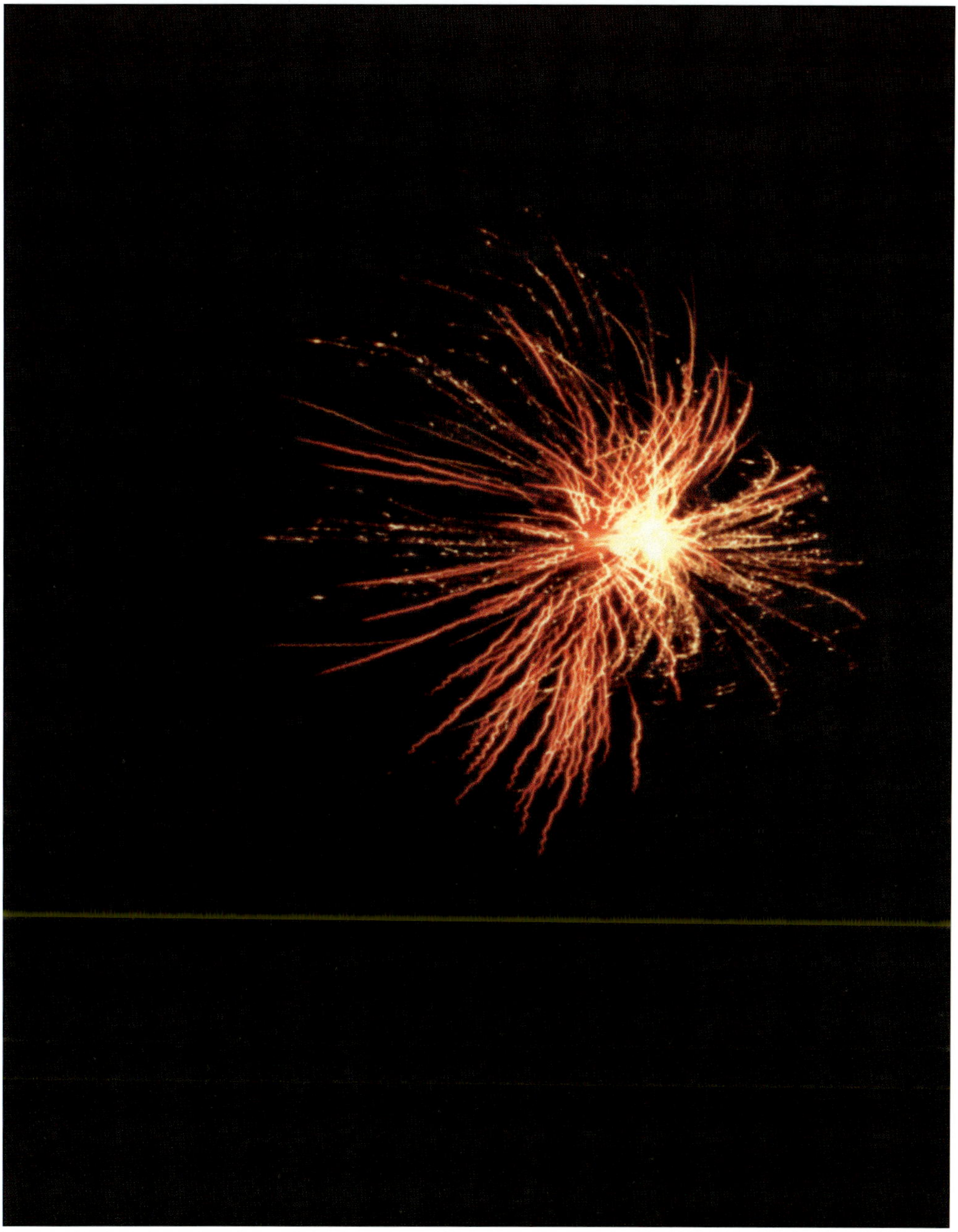

Fireworks light up the sky at Maple Grove Raceway during the 1970s. A crowd always enjoyed fireworks by Fred Spiezio, master pyrotechnist of Fireworks USA in Pottstown. Spiezio also shared his love of fireworks at Manatawny Park (during Fourth of July events), the Reading Fairgrounds, and many more locations. (Courtesy of Fred Spiezio.)

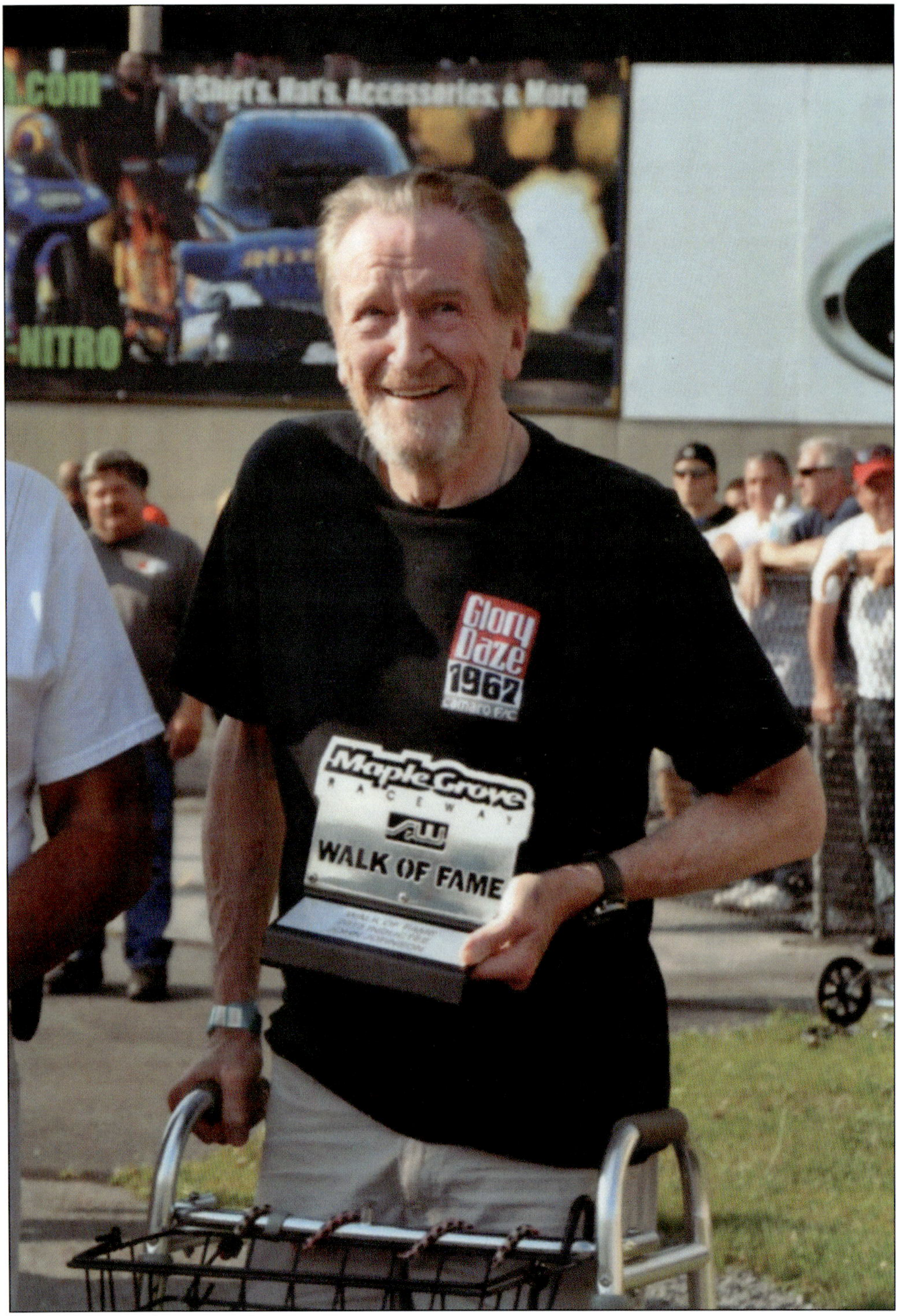

John Johnson was inducted into the Maple Grove Raceway Walk of Fame in 2013. Johnson was thrilled to be honored at Maple Grove, where he spent much of his life. His family was there to support him on this special day. (Courtesy of John Johnson.)

Four

Grandview Speedway

Catch Me If You Can

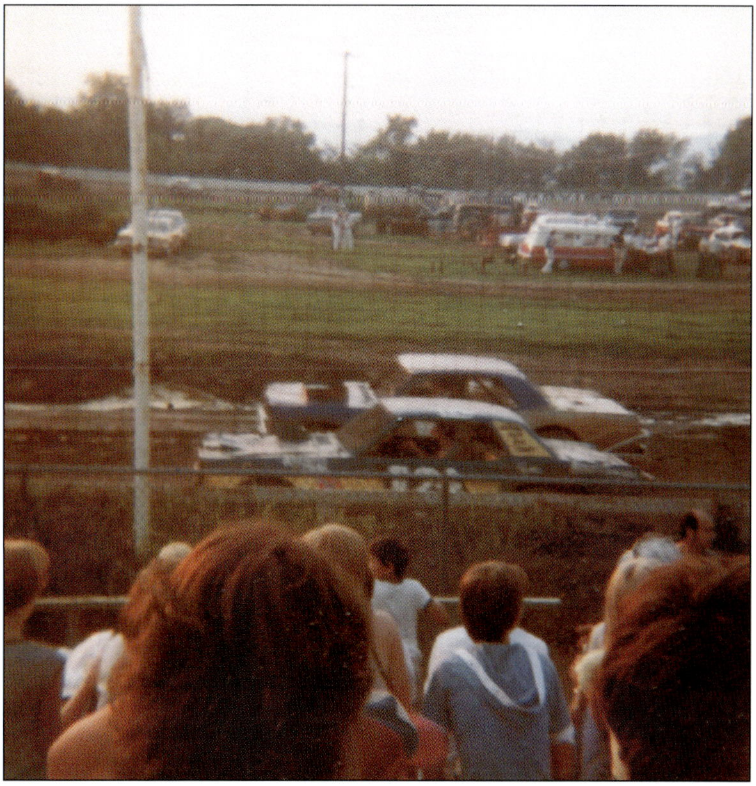

Louie Thompson is in No. 124 during the 1980s at Grandview Speedway in a picture that depicts racing in that era. The background reveals the need for equipment that helps the show continue to run smoothly. The crowd looks on as they wait for results of the race. (Courtesy of Charles Grebe Jr.)

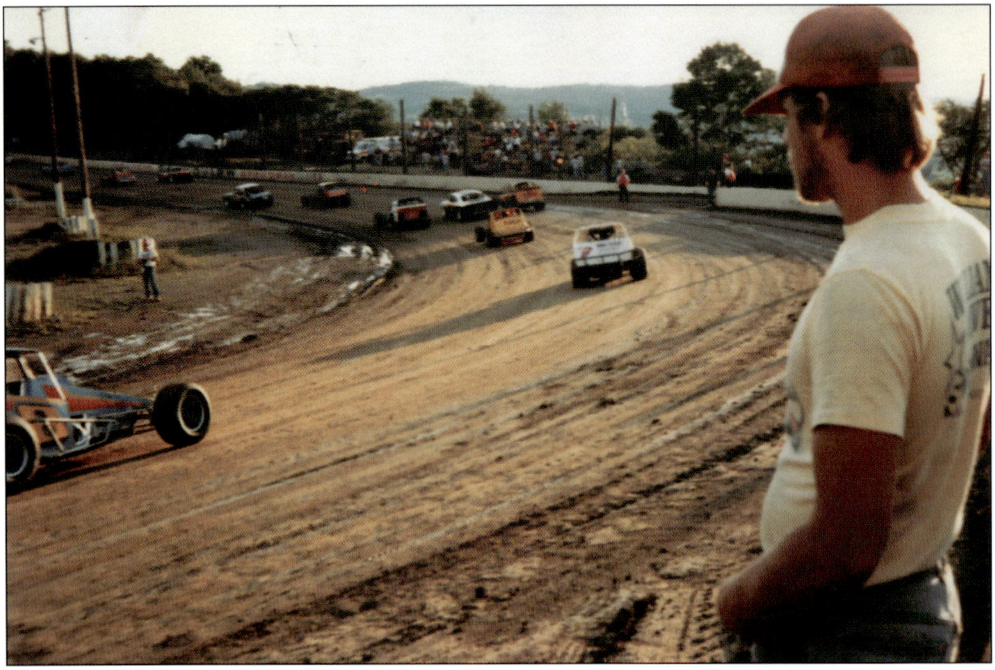

Over the years, many men and women have worked at Grandview Speedway; Glenn Mertz worked as pit steward and in traffic control, Joe Jordan welded tires, and Ernie Saxton was the announcer for many years. Female drivers—such as Kelly Snyder (No. 102) and Amanda Spots (No. 79)—have also made their marks. (Both, courtesy of Joe Jordan.)

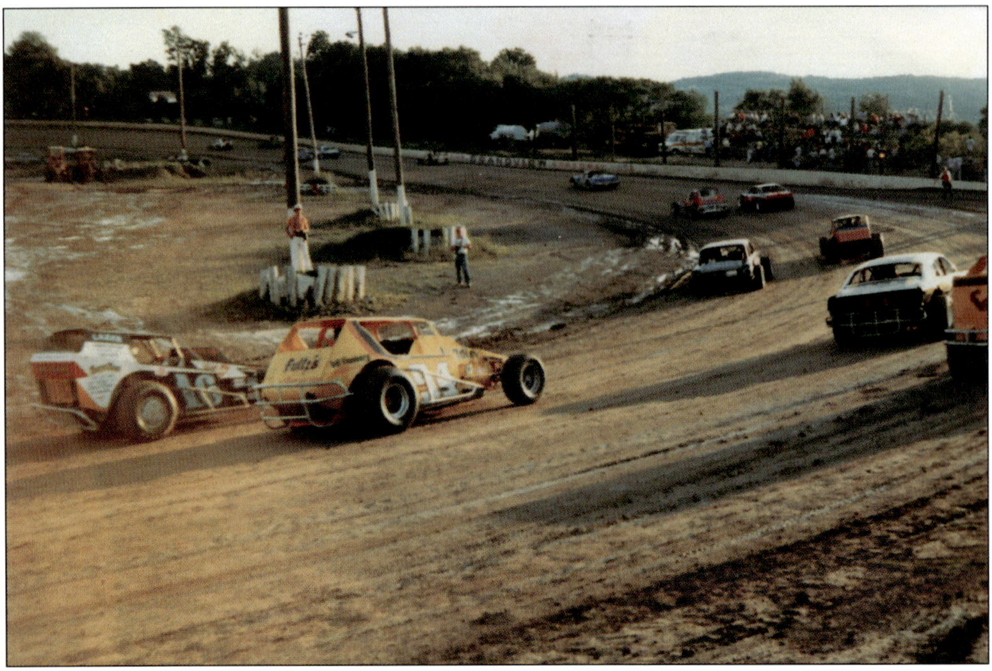

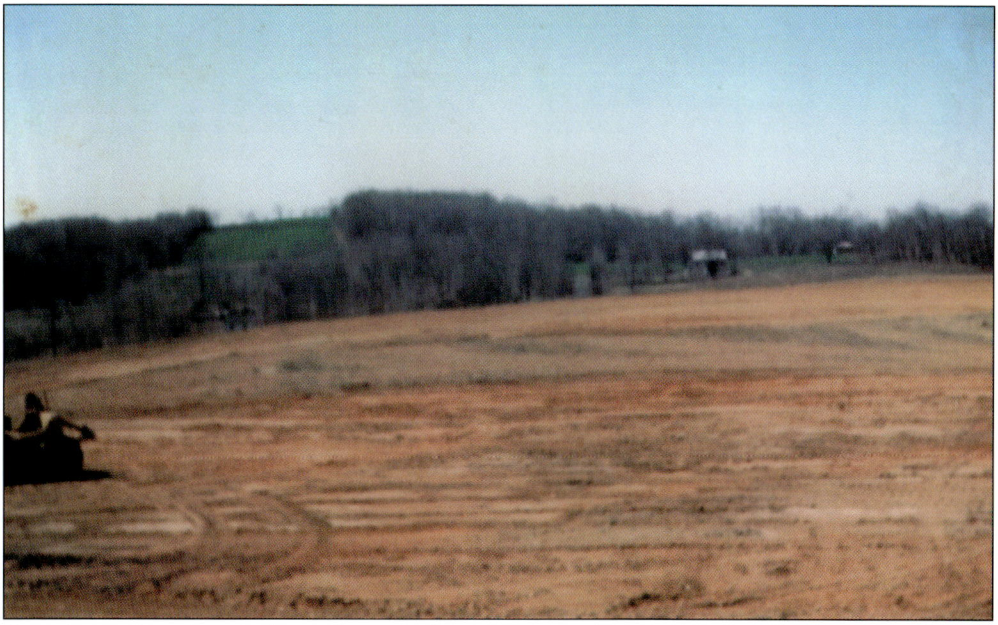

Grandview Speedway is located in Washington Township, Berks County, near Bechtesville, Pennsylvania. In 1962, Forest Rodgers, his family, and several workers broke ground on the speedway. It is a one-third-mile race track featuring high banks and a wide surface for racing. It is good for passing and closed racing. The track was originally planned to be a quarter-mile asphalt track in Pottstown. Over the years, Grandview has undergone many changes to improve the track and the facilities on the premise. Fans fill the grandstands to support their favorite drivers and listen to the roar of the cars from the pits to the track. It has always been a love of racing, no matter what job they perform, that keeps the track workers coming back for more, from drivers to concessions workers, ticket takers, flagmen, mechanics, and more. Today, Bruce Rodgers, son of Forest, is the owner of Grandview Speedway. (Both, courtesy of Joe Jordan.)

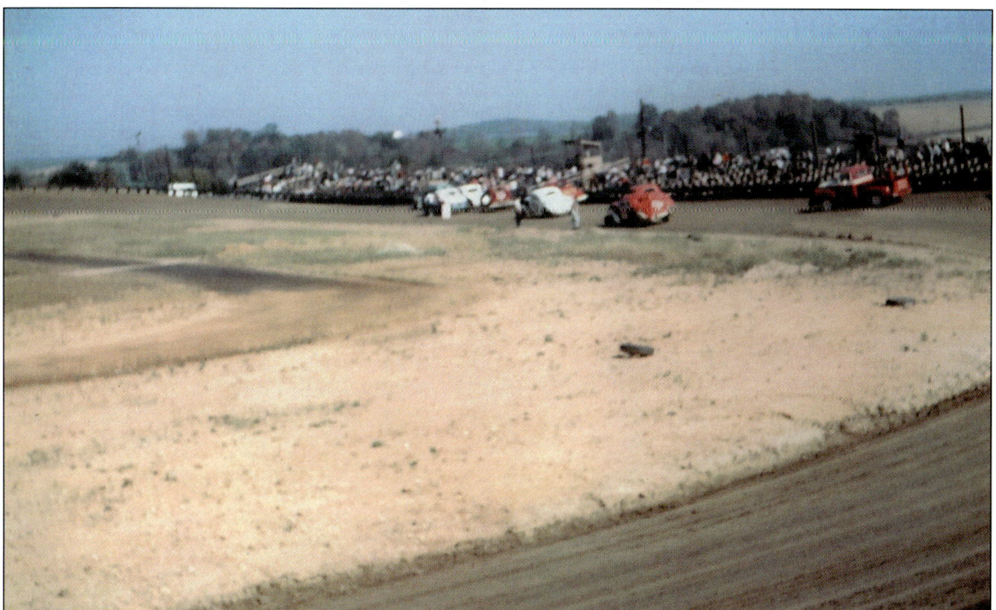

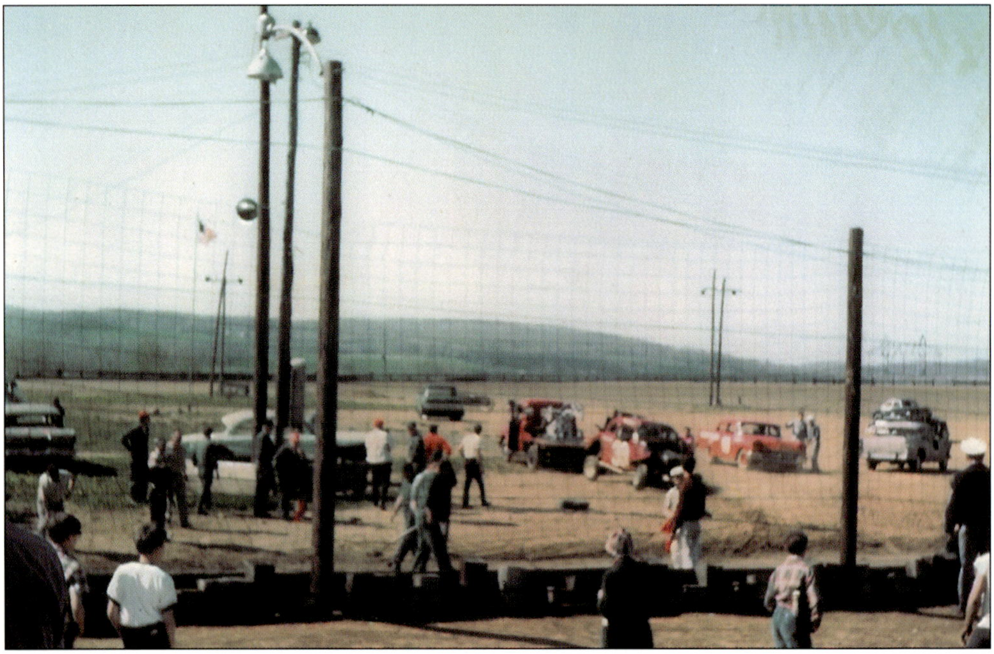

Grandview Speedway has been an exciting place since it opened in 1963. Fans and drivers enjoy this family-run track that caters to its fans. Fans can bring their children to watch and cheer, and each generation can bond through their shared love of racing. (Courtesy of Joe Jordan.)

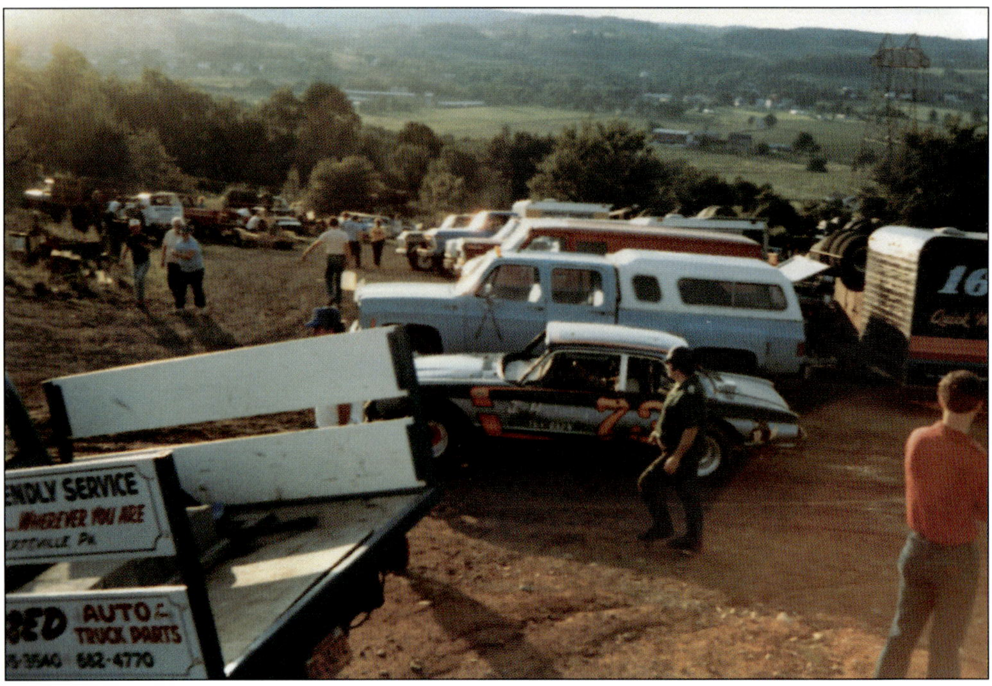

The pit area of Grandview Speedway is shown here in the 1980s. Over the years, the pit area has changed, but not by much. Drivers and crew members are working on cars, getting ready for competition, and spending time with family before and after the race. Each day can be different, with new issues, but the excitement of winning outweighs everything. (Courtesy of Joe Jordan.)

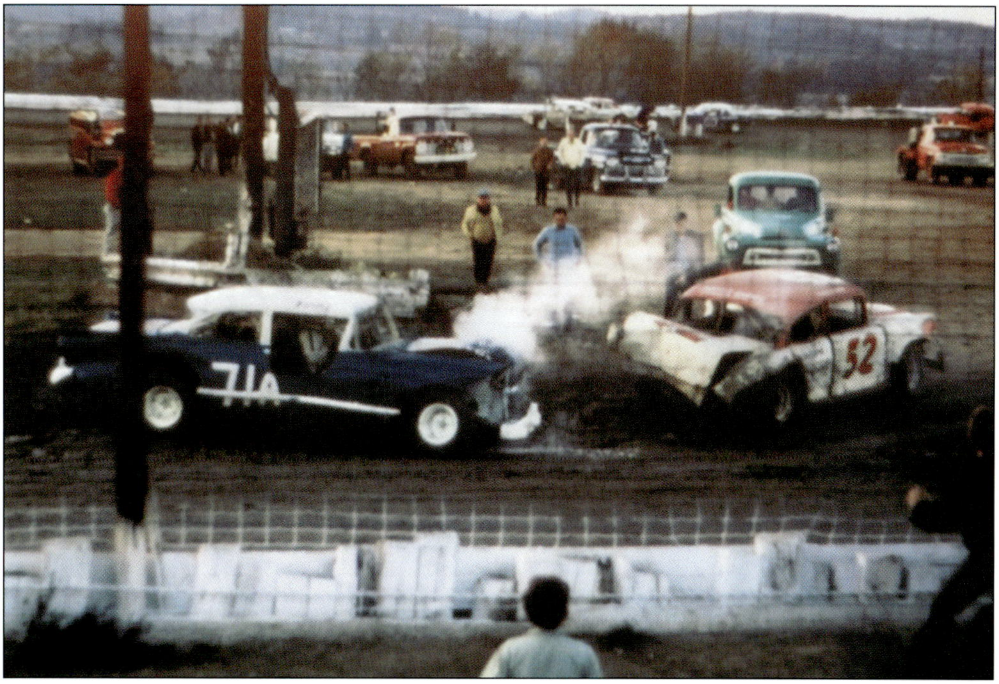

In this 1970s photograph of Grandview Speedway, E.B. Smith (No. 52) is hit by Dave "Sonny" Meslser (No. 71). Meslser's car is owned by Charles Grebe Sr. The crowd and pit crew watch the crash as the rest of the cars make their way around the track. (Courtesy of Charles Grebe Jr.)

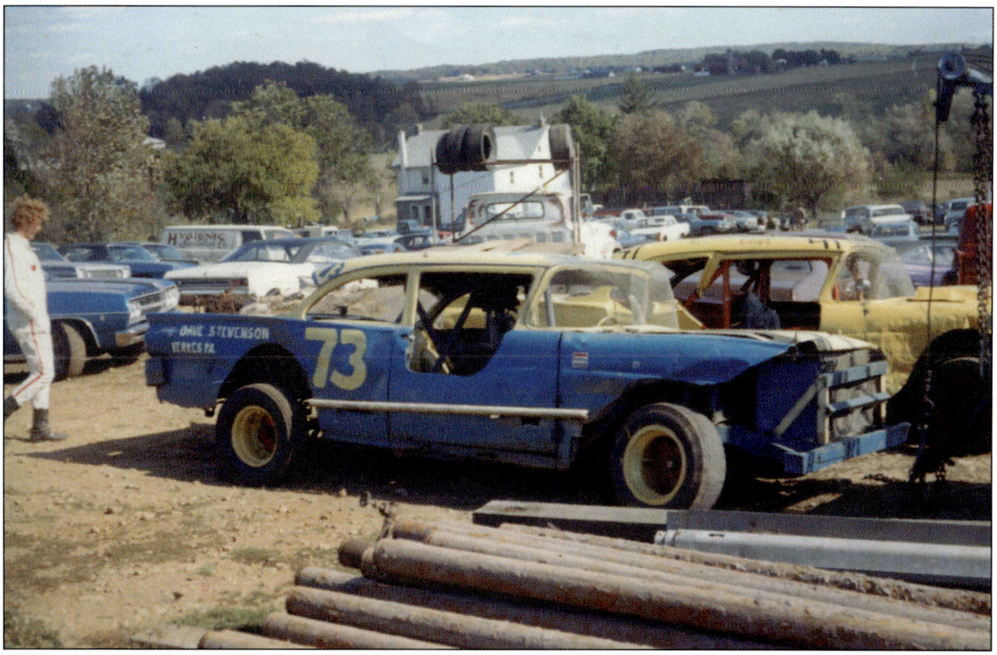

This spectacular view, visible from Grandview Speedway, in shown here the 1960s. Charles Grebe's Chevy, No. 73, is parked in the lot. The 1960s were a great time to race at Grandview, as the track was in its early years, but it has continued to bring great joy to sports fans throughout the years. (Courtesy of Charles Grebe Jr.)

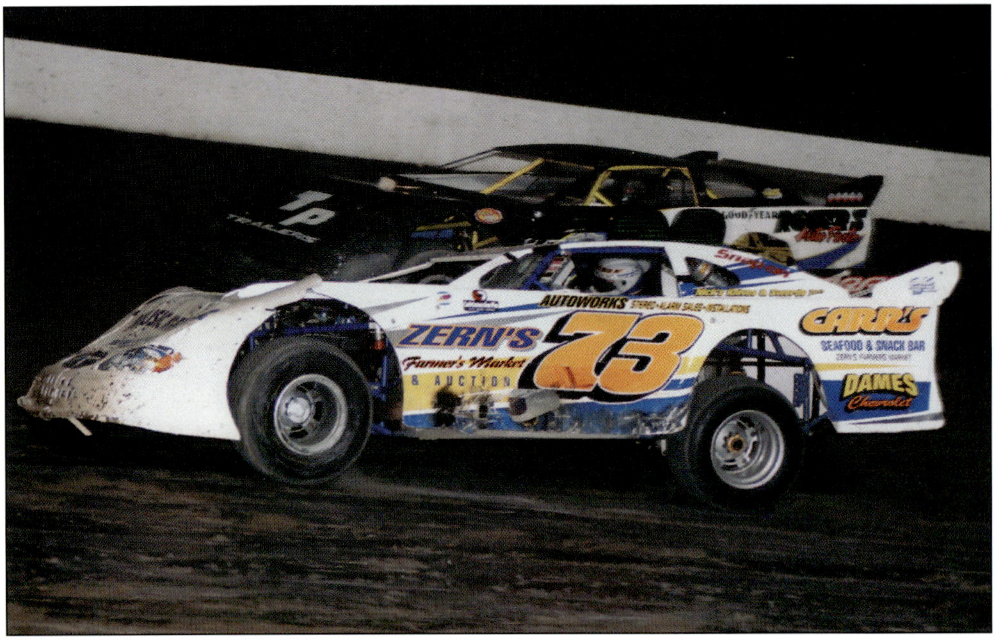

Charles Grebe, of Gilbertsville, Pennsylvania, has been around Grandview Speedway for many years. He drove a late model race car to eight wins at Grandview. He raced from 1973 until 2006. Grebe is still active at the track to this day. (Courtesy of Charles Grebe Jr.)

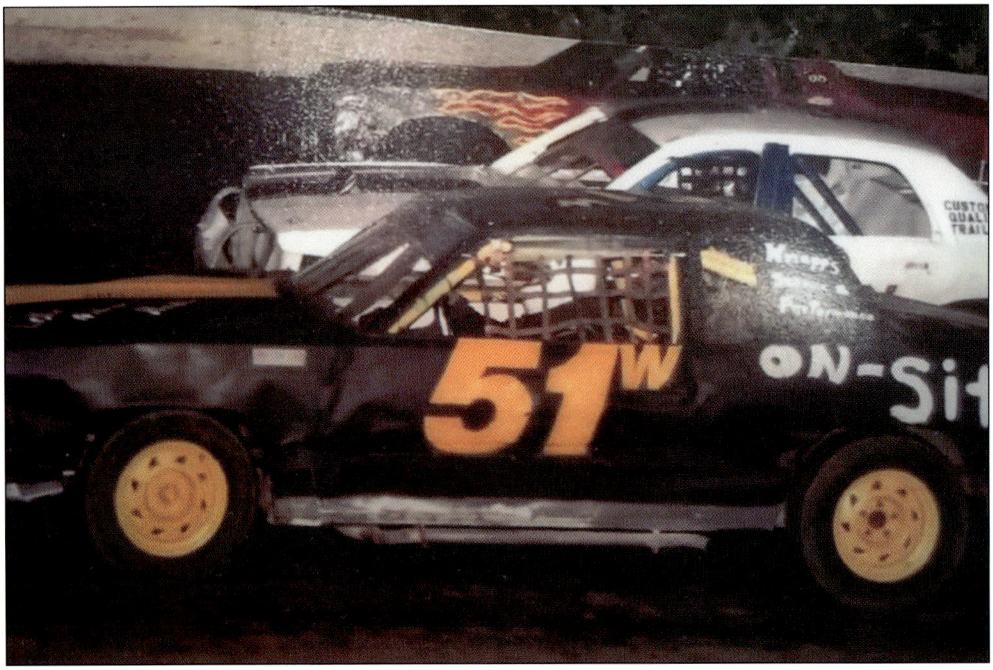

Dunn Wade, of Stowe, Pennsylvania, is shown here racing his 1980s Plymouth Eudora car at Grandview Speedway. He has been racing since the early 1990s. Wade started by racing go-carts with much success. He later started drag racing at Maple Grove Raceway in Friday night grudge races in his 1969 Camaro. He continues to race the Eudora races to this day. (Courtesy of Dunn Wade.)

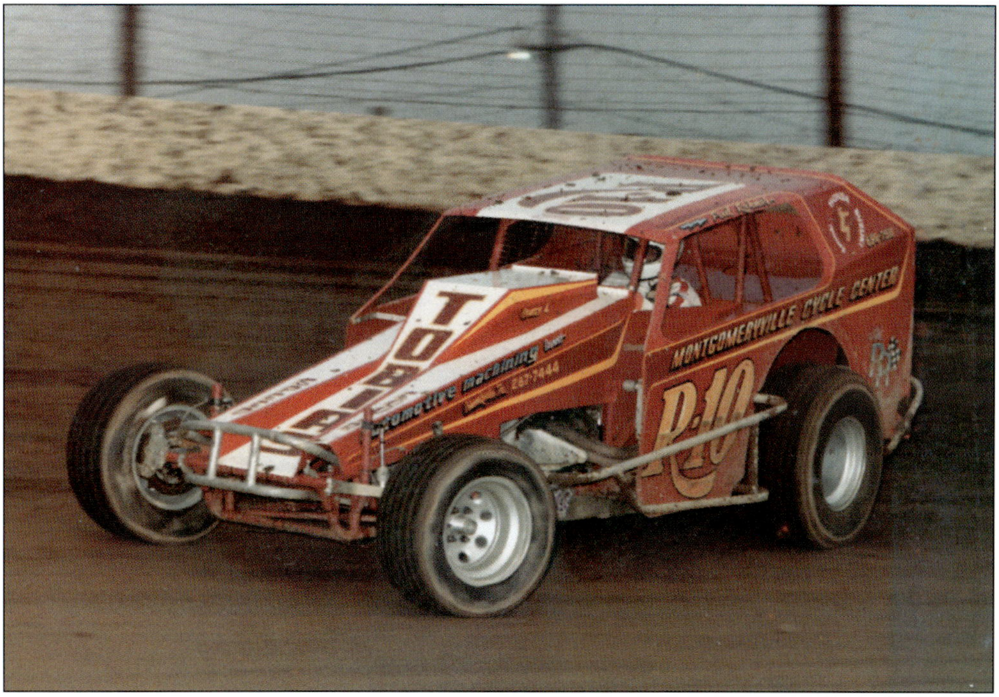

"Fast Freddie" Rhamer was a feature winner in 1983, winning track championships three times in 1983 at Grandview Speedway. He has seven track championship wins at Grandview Speedway alone. Always the man to beat, he is truly a favorite at the track. (Courtesy of Mark Rubright.)

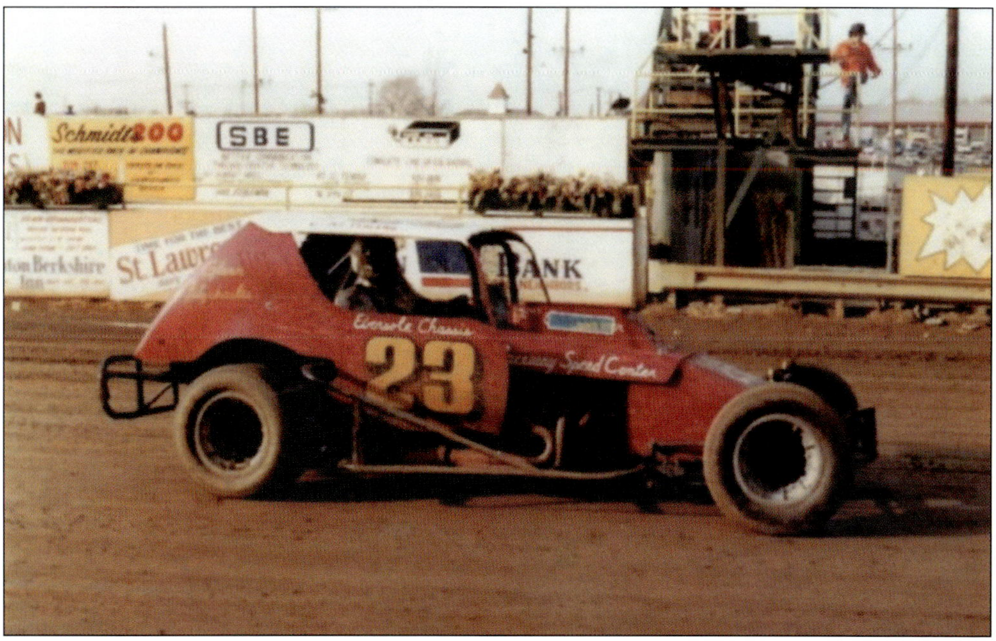

Glenn Fitzcharles, a fierce dirt track and modified stock car driver, is shown here. Fitzcharles's career spanned many years until his retirement in 1999. In 1981, he was the winner of the United Racing Club main event. His last race was at Grandview Speedway, exactly where he won his first race. (Courtesy of Rick Huff Photography.)

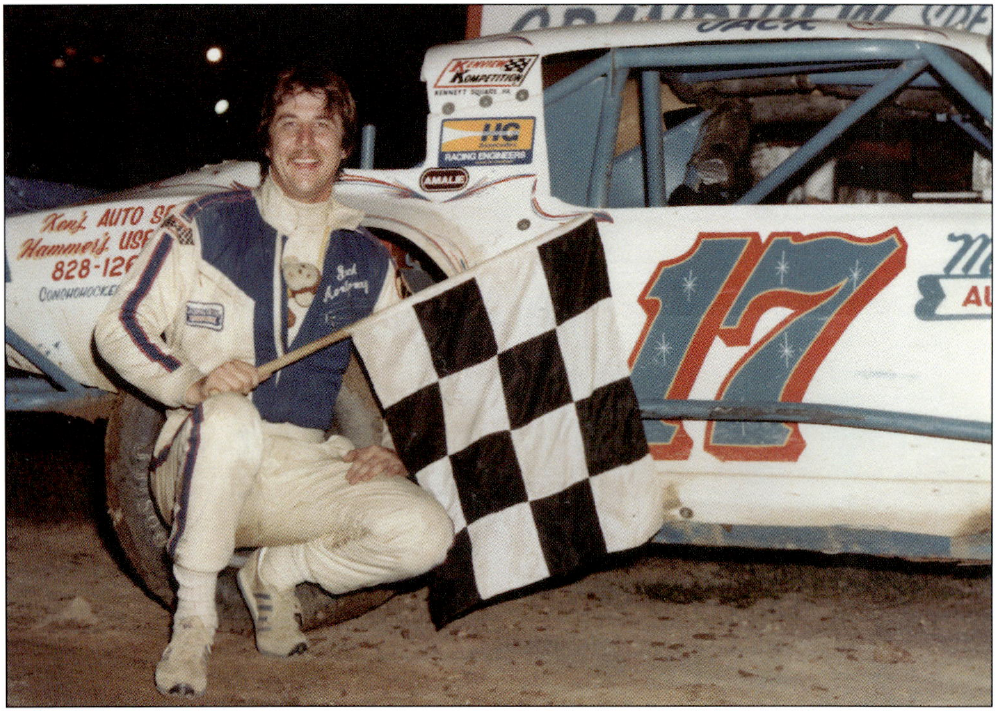

The late Jack Montgomery (No. 17) is shown here at Grandview Speedway in the 1980s. Montgomery was a very popular driver, winning the Firecracker 40 on July 11, 1981. He had 10 wins as a late-model driver and also owned Montgomery Auto Body. (Courtesy of Mark Rubright.)

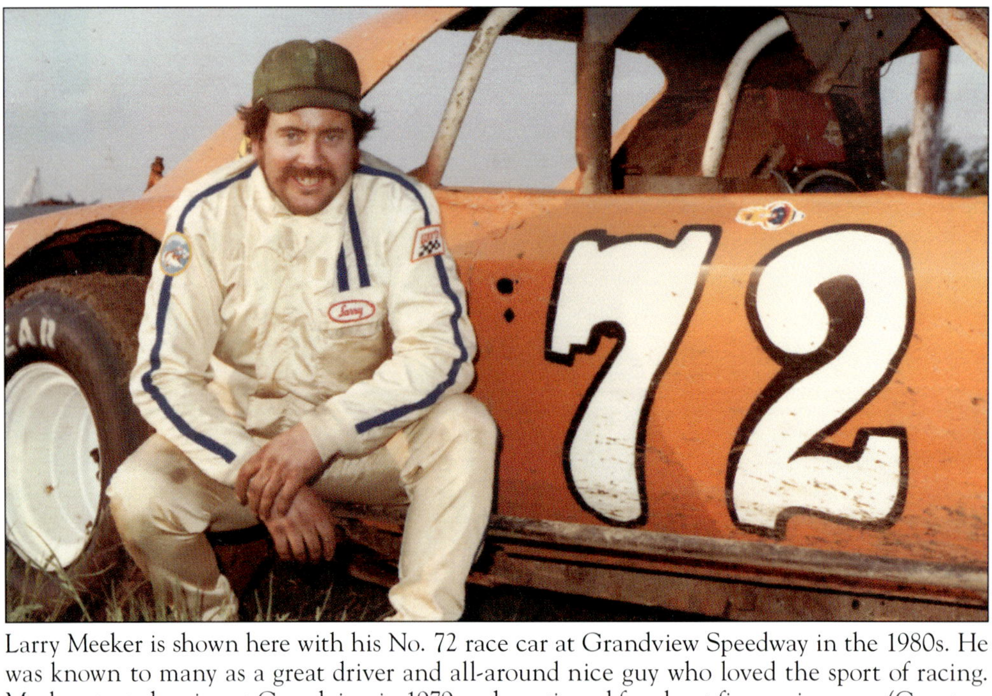

Larry Meeker is shown here with his No. 72 race car at Grandview Speedway in the 1980s. He was known to many as a great driver and all-around nice guy who loved the sport of racing. Meeker started racing at Grandview in 1979 and continued for about five or six years. (Courtesy of Mark Rubright.)

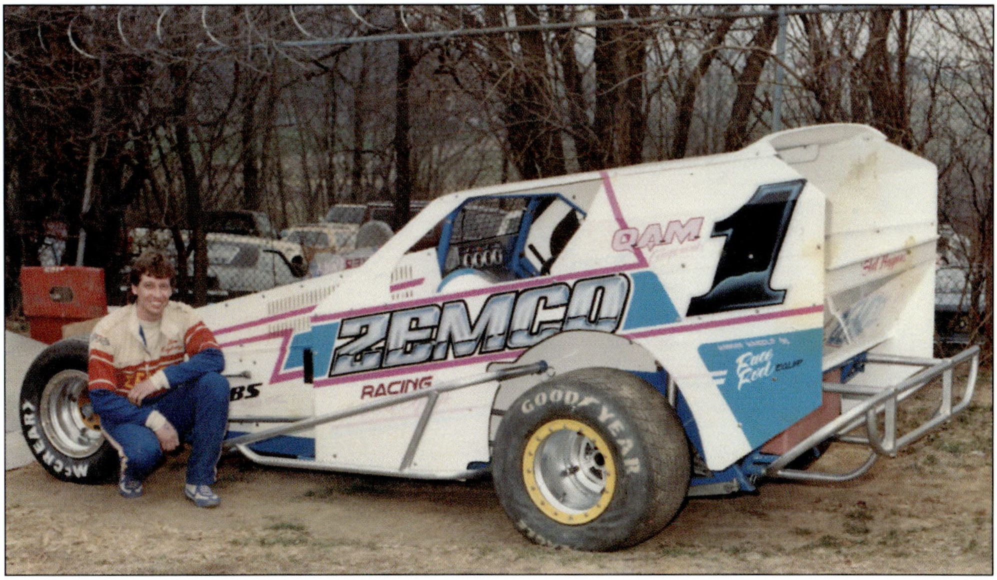

Tom Mayberry, of Sellersville, Pennsylvania, has raced at Grandview Speedway for more than 30 years. He won the track championship in 1991. Mayberry teamed up with former driver Mike Kelly and won the modified championship at Grandview Speedway, and in 1992, they won the high-status Forest Rodgers Memorial in Berks County. Mayberry has had a career of 20 wins at Grandview Speedway alone and has won over 70 feature races. (Courtesy of Charles Grebe Jr.)

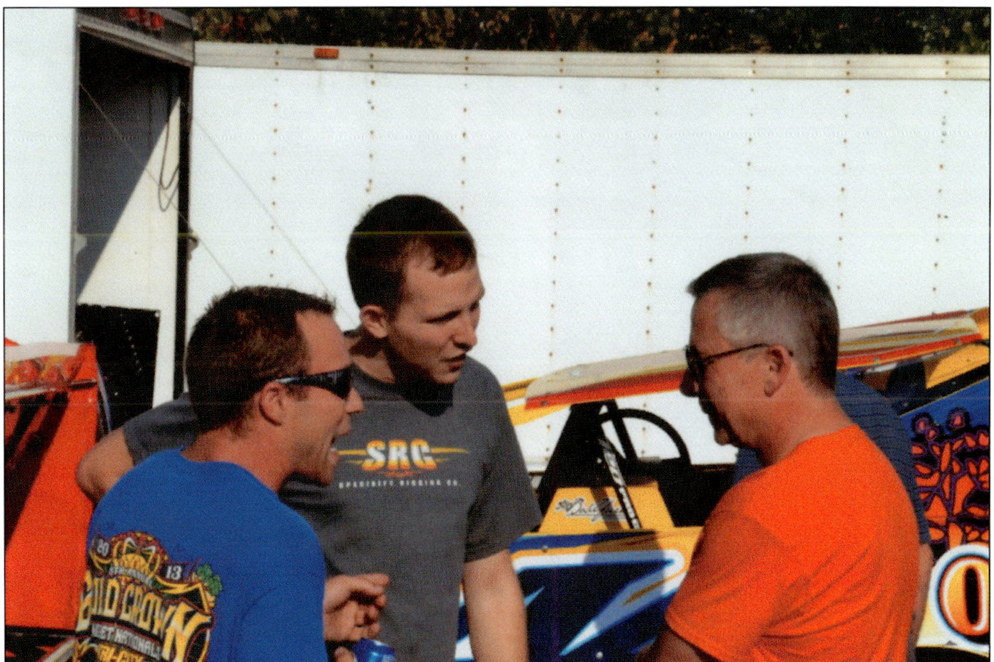

Tim Backwater (left), Billy Pauch Jr. (center), and Billy Pauch Sr. talk racing in the pit area at Grandview Speedway on September 19, 2015. The pit area is always full of conversation and hard work, and decisions need to be quickly made before and during each race. Each moment counts due to accuracy and speed. (Courtesy of SDS Photography.)

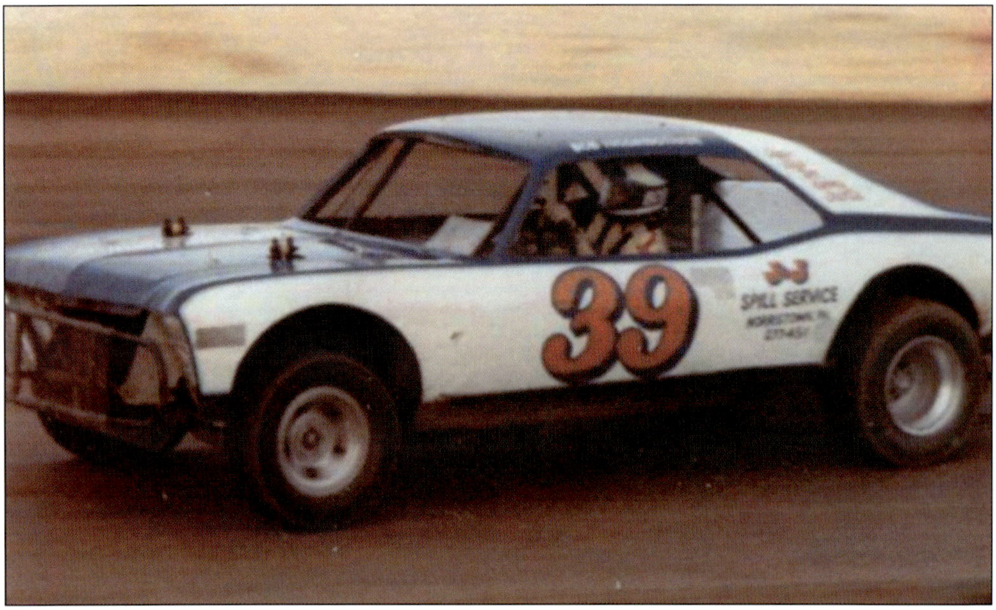

Bob Higginbotham drove the No. 39 at Grandview Speedway and the Reading Fairground Speedway. It was owned by Sam Worthton and family, from Hatfield, Pennsylvania. In 1971–1972, Higginbotham owned his own late model, the "Big Bad Blue," which he named after the color of the paint used on his car. The paint was made by American Motors. He became the track champion without a feature win at Grandview Speedway in 1973. (Courtesy of Charles Grebe Jr.)

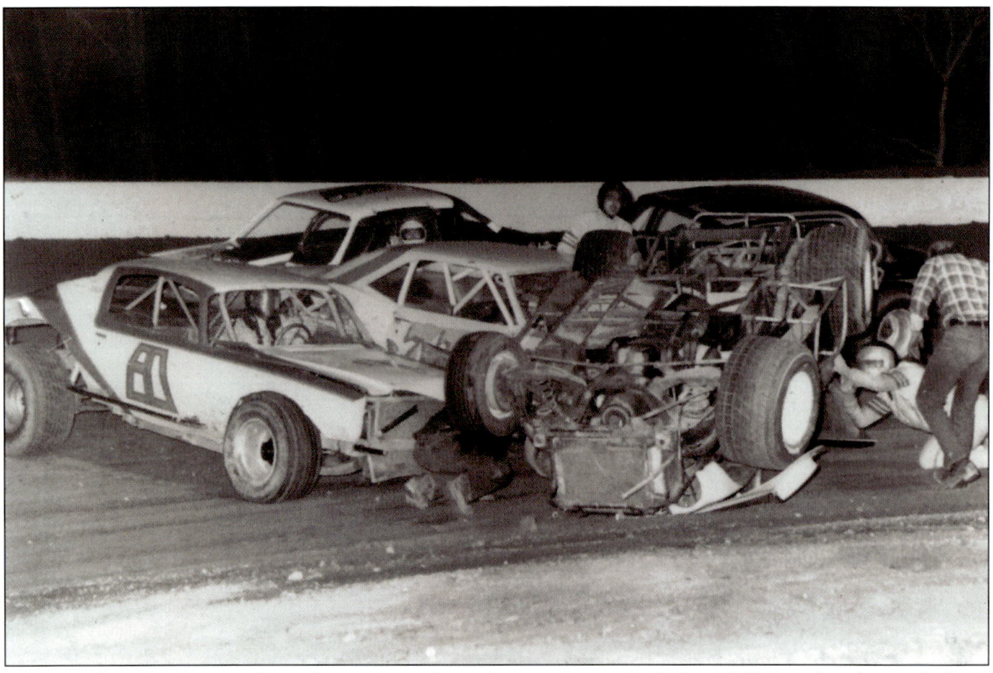

This crash took place at Grandview Speedway during the mid-1980s. Will Smith is being helped out of his car by Charles Grebe Jr. of Boyertown. Drivers and crew have helped during dangerous car wrecks, and the safety of the drivers and fans are of the utmost importance in the racing community. Safety gear is always a must in this type of sport. (Courtesy of Charles Grebe Jr.)

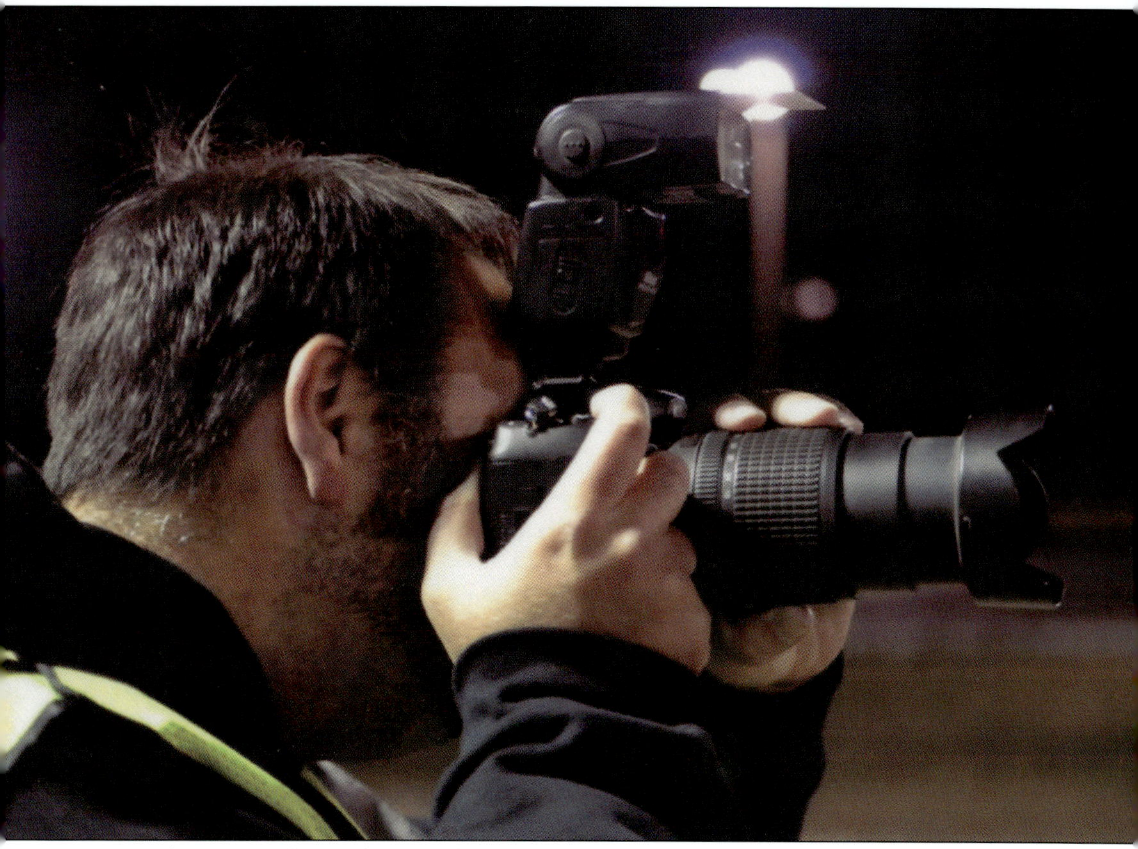

Steve D. Sabo, owner of SDS Photography, really enjoys his time working at Grandview Speedway as a track photographer. Sabo has been watching the races since the early 1990s at Grandview Speedway and made frequent visits to Nazareth Speedway and Dorney Park's asphalt track. He often visited the pits at Grandview to take pictures of the action, which led him to photography, which has been his full-time career for the last two and a half years. Steve and his wife, Sandy Quintus Sabo, have introduced their four-year-old daughter, Abby, to racing. They started bringing her to the track when she was just one year old to watch the free practice sessions at the beginning of the year. Abby enjoys watching and learning about the cars and is now able to stay longer before falling asleep. (Courtesy of SDS Photography.)

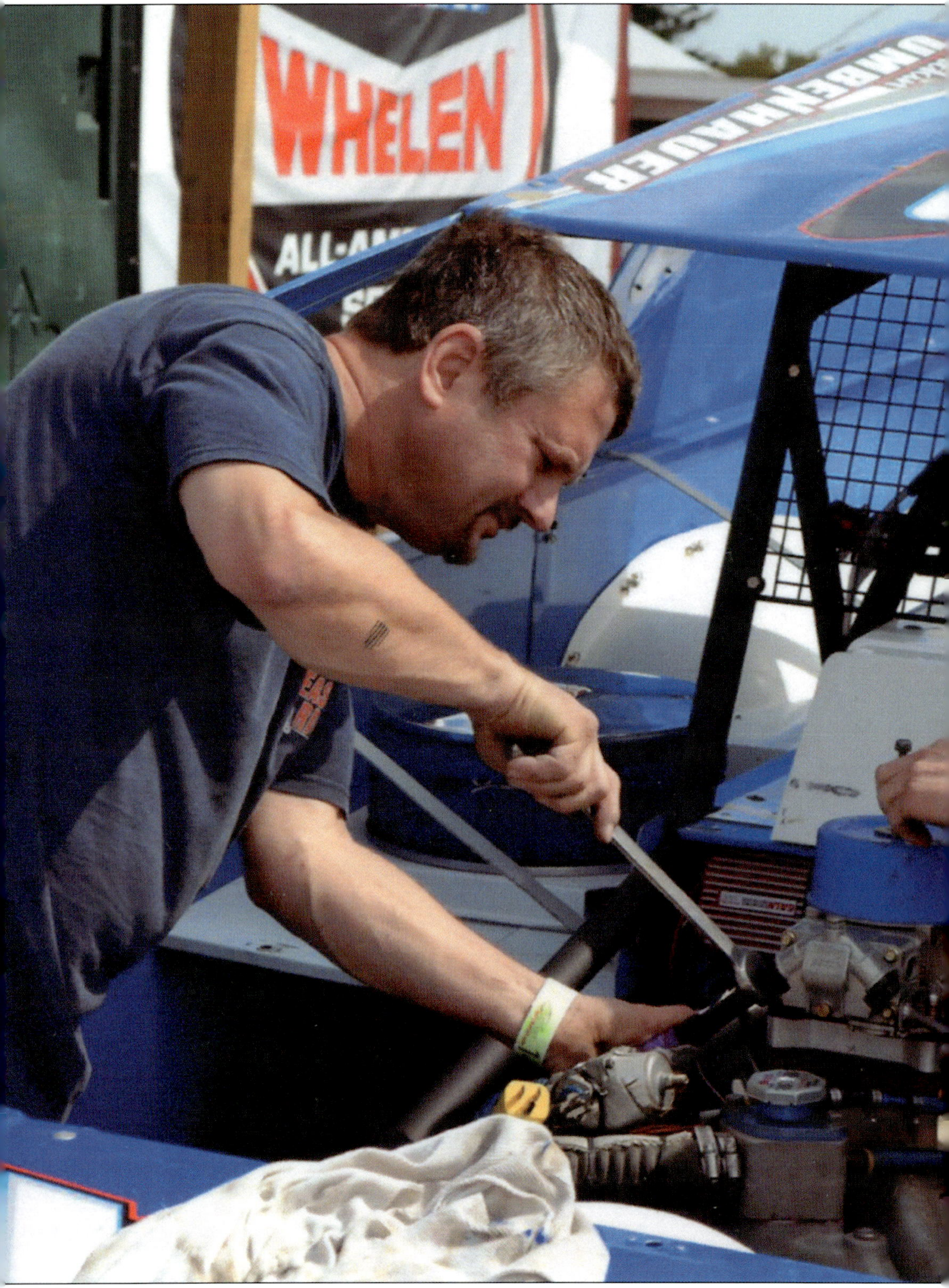
WHELEN

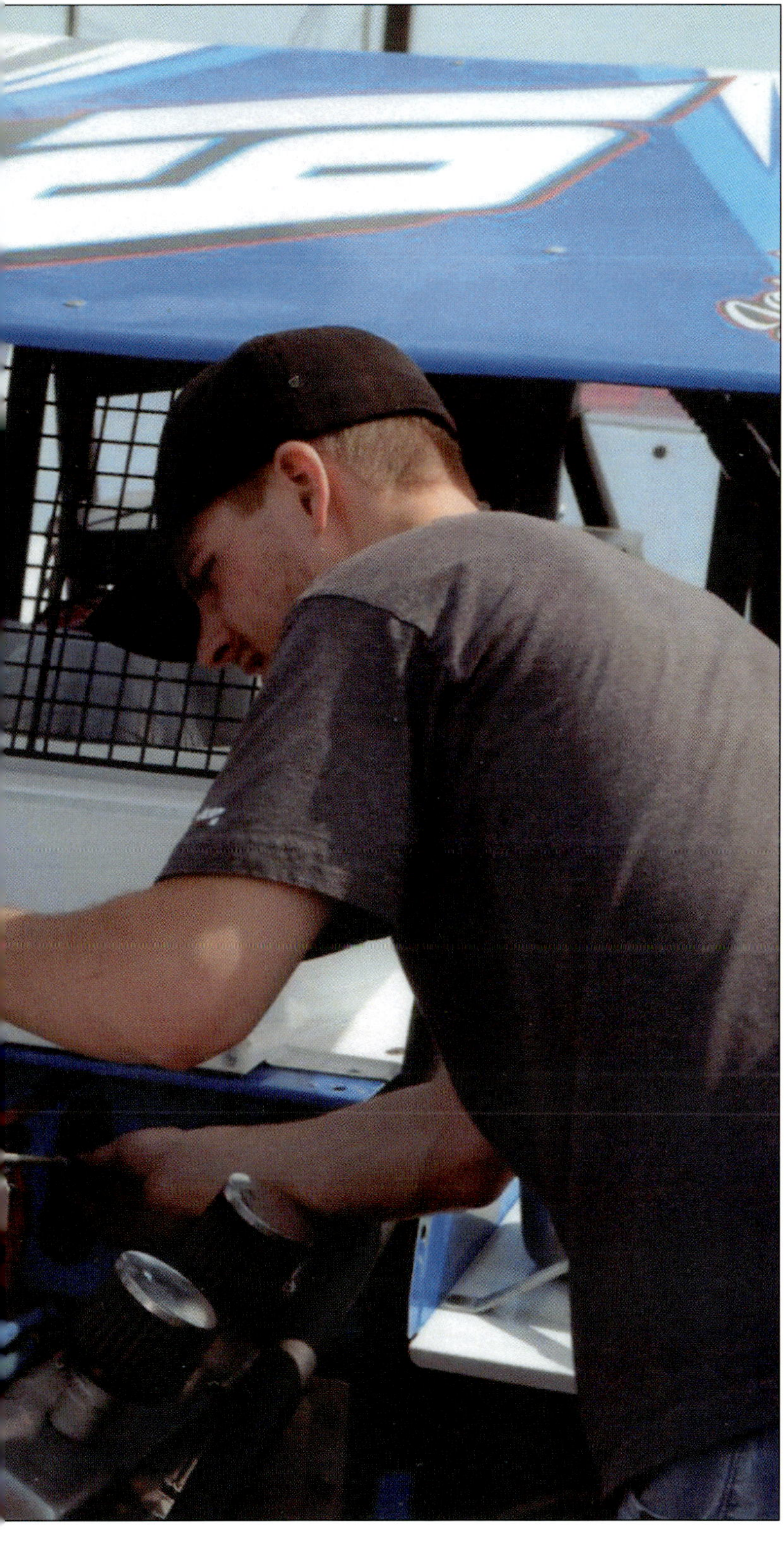

Tom Umbenhauer (left) helps his oldest son, Jordan, go through Freedom 76 pre-tech on September 20, 2014. Tom is the founder of Umbenhauer Motorsports, which was established in 1986. He has been racing through the divisions from street stock car to a Sportsman Modified. Jordan has followed in his father's footsteps by racing small-block and Sportsman Modified cars. (Courtesy of SDS Photography.)

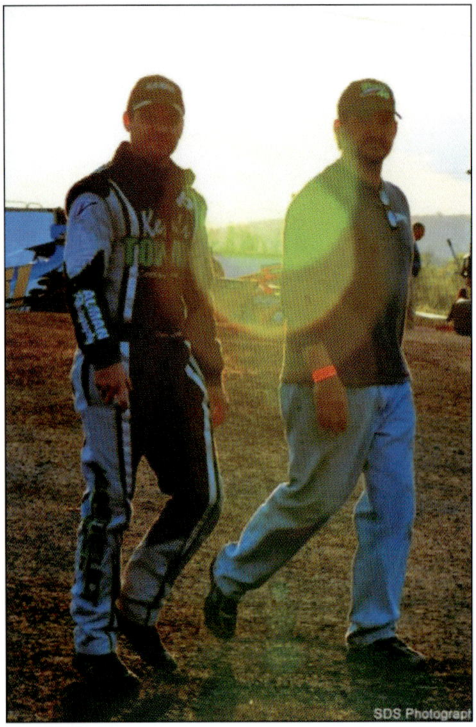

Dan Green (No. 46), of G&H Motorsports, is shown here in the pits with his cousin Brett Higginbotham (right) in 2015. Green has been driving late models for 22 years and runs Saturday nights at Grandview Speedway. In 2013, Green became the Grandview Speedway Late Model Rookie of the Year after an amazing season, which included five top-10 finishes. Green started racing go-carts at age 13 in 1993 at Shell Hammer's Speedway in Leesport, Pennsylvania. Higginbotham works on Green's pit crew and is an administrator of the team's Facebook page and www.DanGreen46.com. (Courtesy of SDS Photography.)

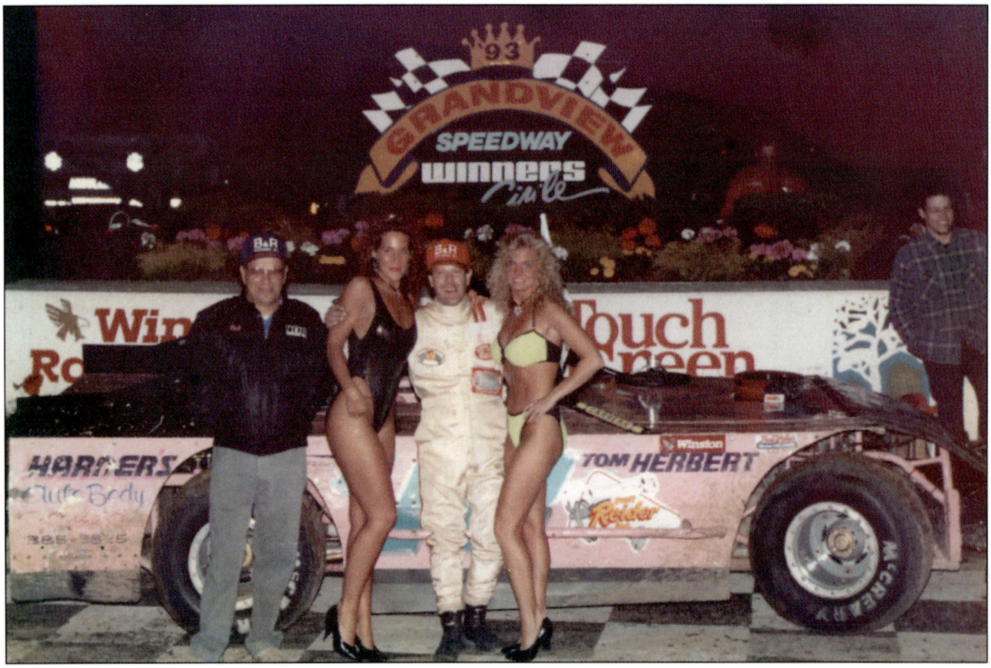

Tom Herbert (November 17, 1949–October 15, 2013), a racing veteran at Grandview Speedway, is pictured posing in the winner's circle in 1993. He drove the "Pink Panther" (No. 18), a 1969 Camaro, in the late model completion. Herbert raced against legends such as Ron Peck (driving "XL2") and Hack Jones (driving "Woody Wood Pecker Special Delivery"). Herbert is often mentioned as a fan favorite in the sport of racing. (Courtesy of Charles Grebe Jr.)

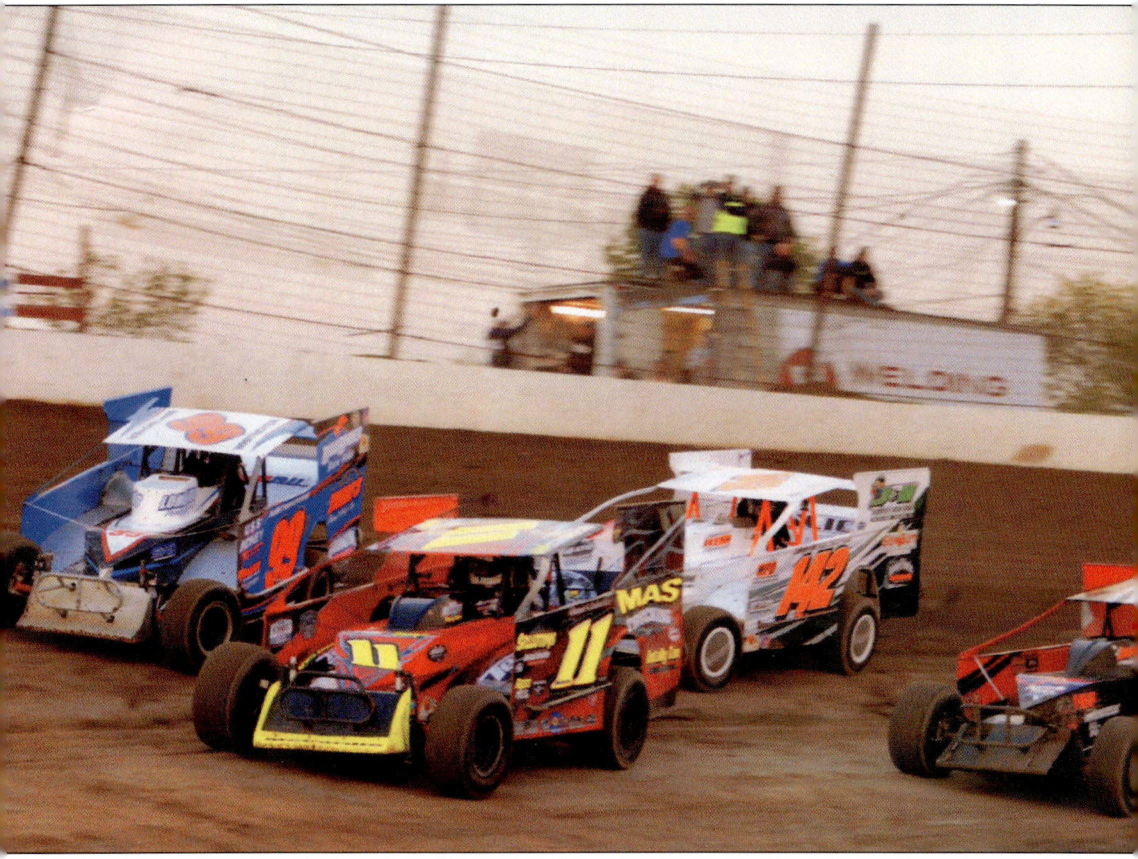

Katie McCardle (No. 11), Brandon Whitmoyer (No. 99 B), Ryan Lillick (No. 142), and Joseph Funk (No. 14 J) race for a qualifying spot during the heat race for Sportsman Modified on May 17, 2014. This was an exciting night of racing that can purchased on DVD at Grandview Speedway. Many fans love to rewatch the race (or watch it for the first time, if they were not able to make it to the race). (Courtesy of SDS Photography.)

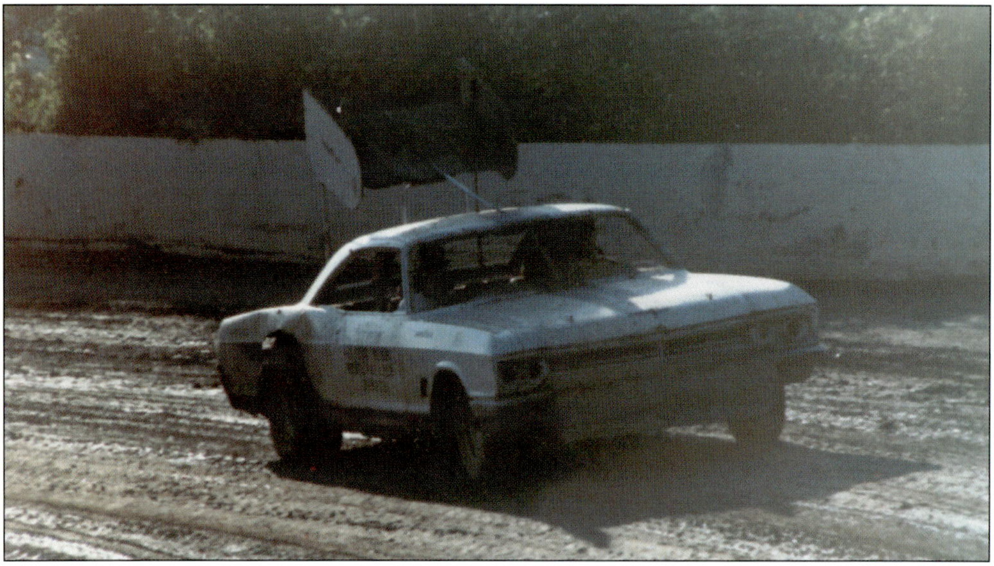

Push cars and trucks help keep Grandview Speedway running smoothly. They are there when a driver needs help getting a car started or to assist with getting the car off the track after an accident—as long as the car is still on four wheels. Push trucks are also used to start sprint cars, since they do not have starters. (Courtesy of Joe Jordan.)

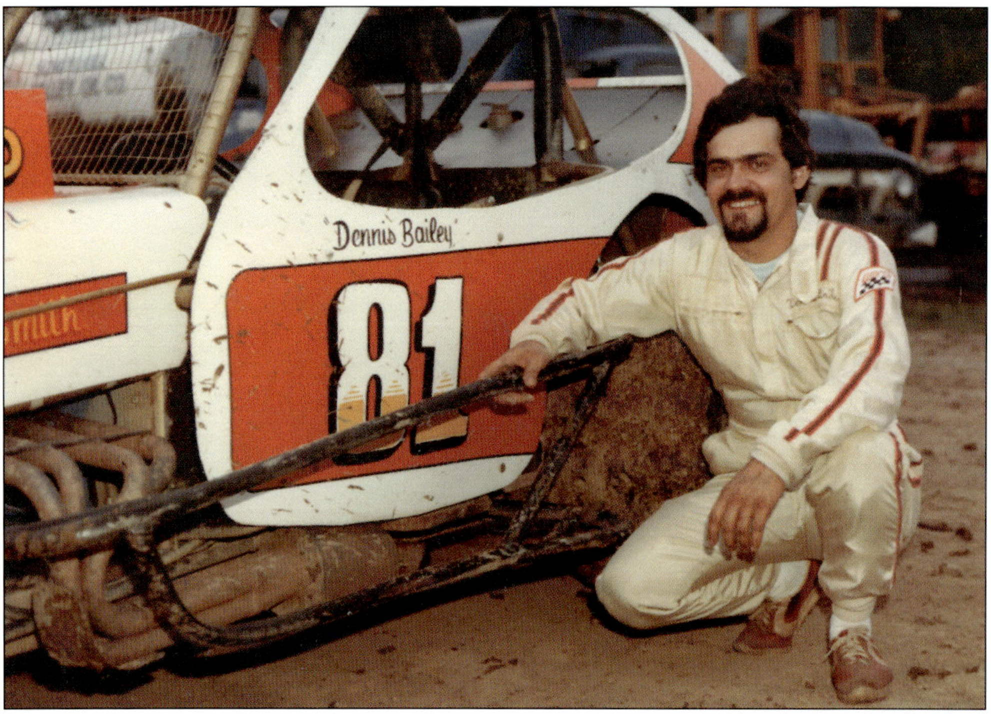

Dennis "Chico" Bailey, shown at Grandview Speedway in the 1980s, has always been a fan favorite. Bailey started his career in 1970 at Dorney Park Speedway with his brother Randy joining him with the No. 80 car. Mike Bailey, Dennis's nephew, also drove the famous No. 81 at Grandview Speedway. In January 2016, the "Bailey bunch" won the Junie Donlavey Spirit of the Sport award at the Eastern Motorsport Press Association convention. (Courtesy of Mark Rubright.)

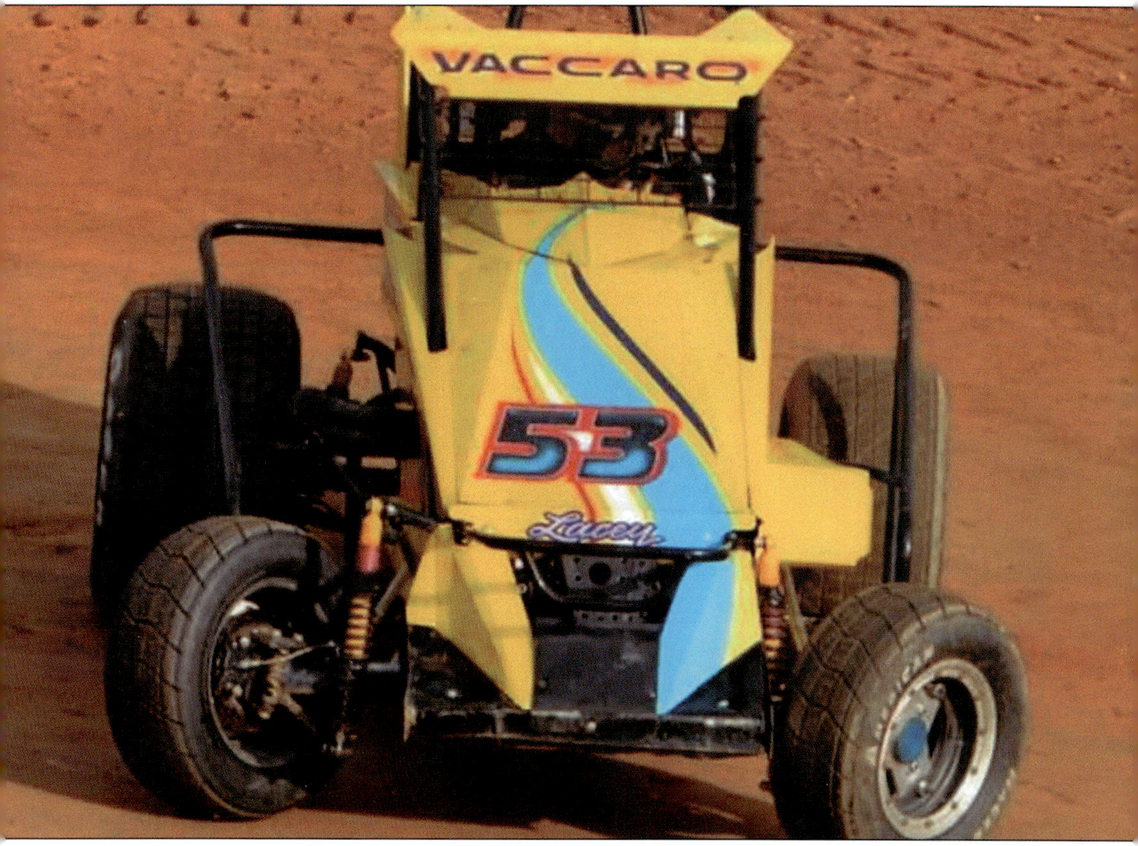

Joseph F. Vaccaro Jr. is shown here at Grandview Speedway during the Fall Jamboree held on October 31 and November 1 in 2015. This event was run by Action Track USA. Vaccaro's family has been racing on and off through the years. Joseph Vaccaro Sr. drove street stocks and modified cars, and his grandson Joey presently runs a Tobias Slingshot. The family always has fun together while teaching Joey the sport of racing. (Courtesy of SDS Photography.)

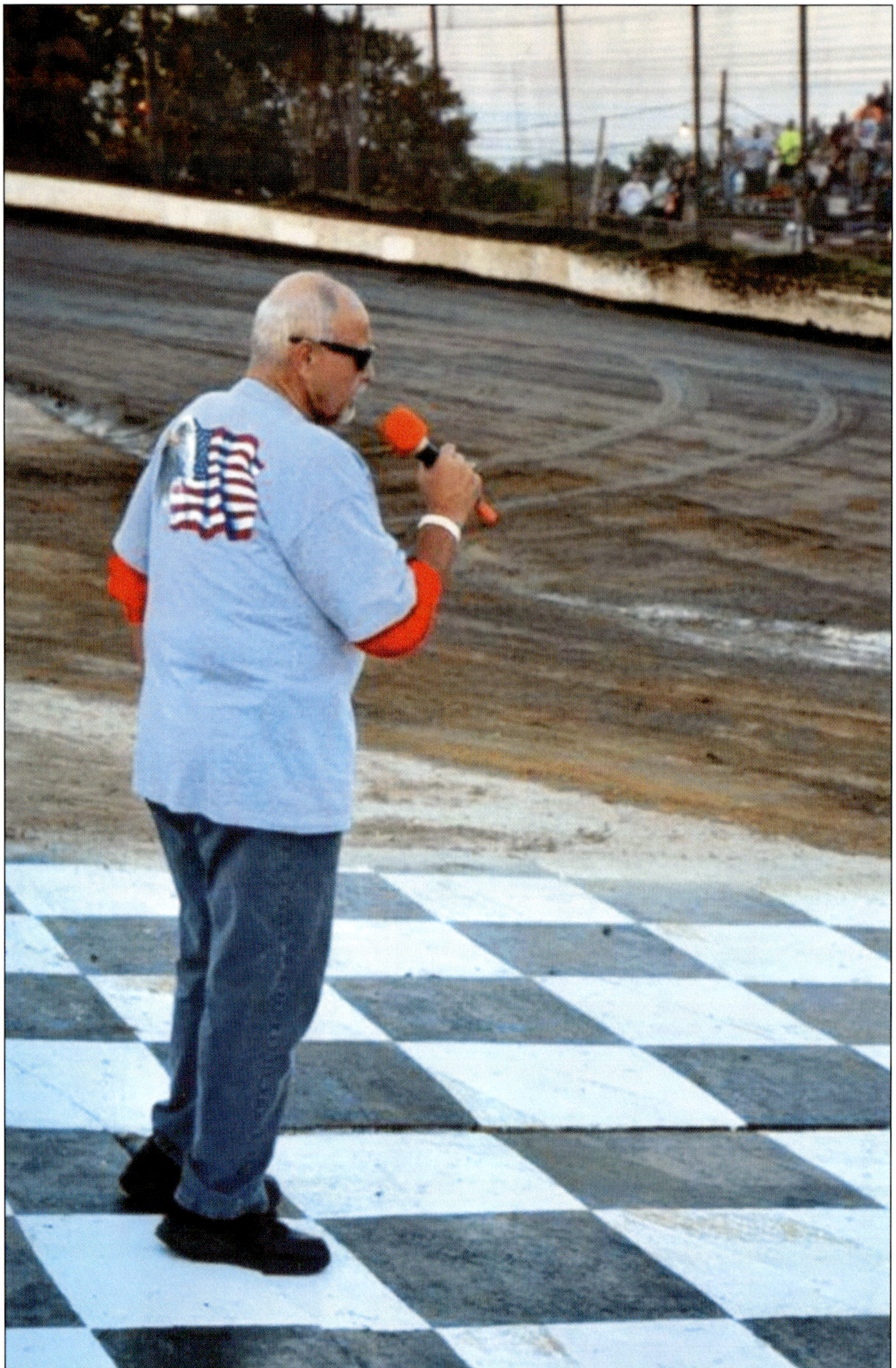

Keith Gerhart sang "The Star-Spangled Banner" during the Firecracker 40 for late models at Grandview Speedway on July 4, 2015. Gerhart has sung "God Bless America," the national anthem, and other patriotic songs at many sporting events in the area. In 2010, he became Grandview Speedway's regular singer. (Courtesy of SDS Photography.)

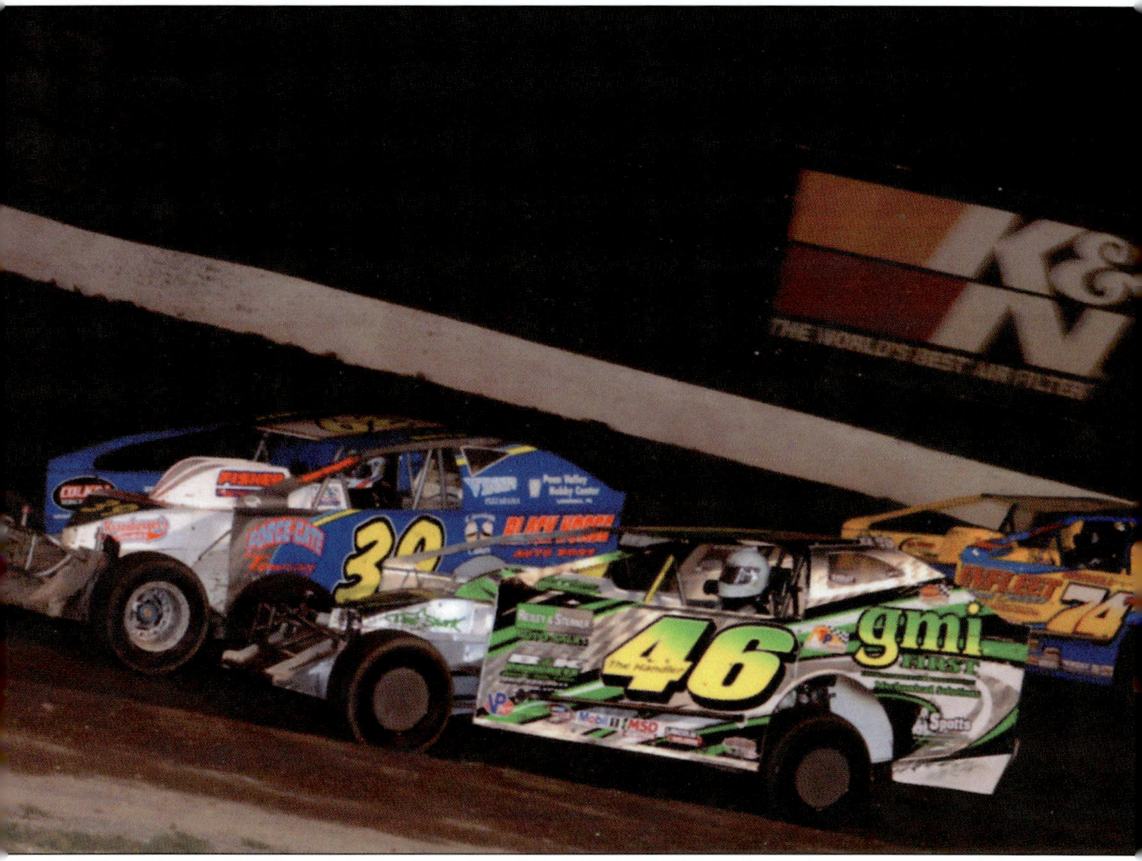

Todd Smith (No. 39), Doug Manmiller (No. 46), and John Willman (No. 74) race for the qualifying position on September 9, 2014. Fans can watch the races on RCN TV, which shows dirt track stock car races. The races are exciting and fun to watch from home or at the track. (Courtesy of SDS Photography.)

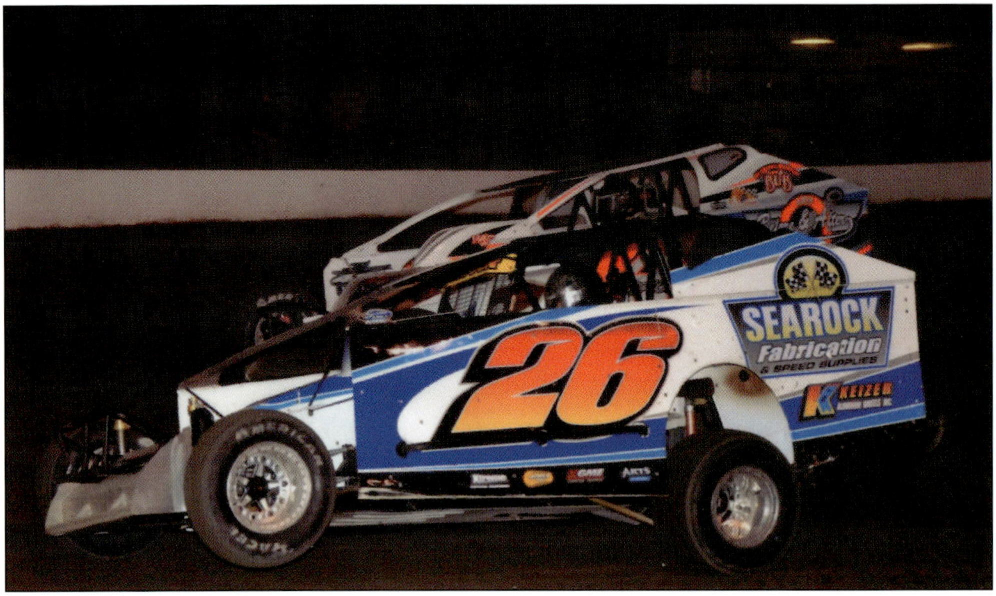

Ryan Grim (No. 26) and Kyle Borror (No. 4) battle for position during the modified feature event on August 8, 2015, at Grandview Speedway. Grim earned his first NASCAR 358 modified win on May 2, 2015. Grim's family has been racing for many years; his grandfather Alfred, his uncle Gary, and his cousins Justin and Brad have all raced at Grandview Speedway. Borror, from Peach Bottom, has been racing for several years now. He is well known for his racing and the interesting paint job on his car. (Courtesy of SDS Photography.)

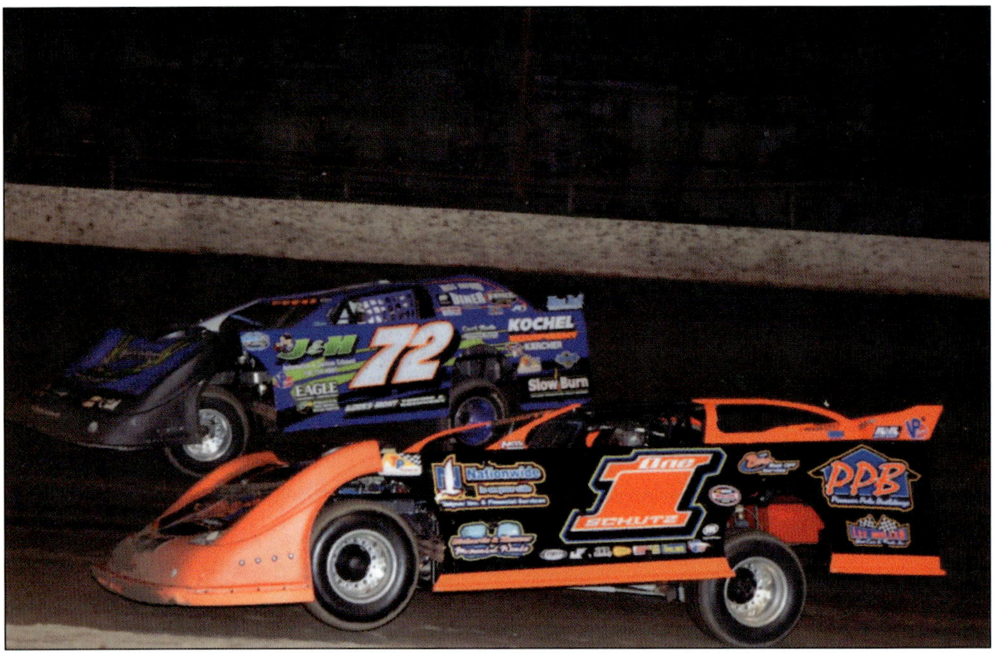

Chuck Schutz (No. 1) battles Wayne Pfeil (No. 72) for the lead during the late model feature on July 4, 2015, at Grandview Speedway. They both made the top five in late model points. Schutz won first place with 4,116 points. Pfeil took second place with 4,027 points, which made for a fantastic season in 2015. (Courtesy of SDS Photography.)

Five

Reading Fairgrounds Speedway

Always Making the Turn

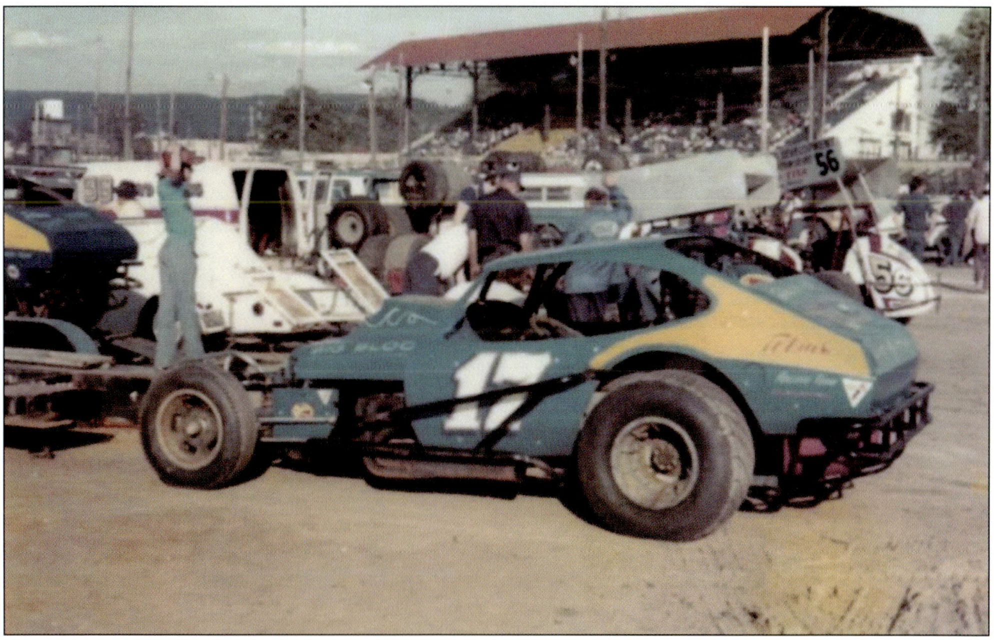

Dick "Toby" Tobias was an outstanding dirt track modified stock car and sprint driver. He was well known for his history at local tracks in 1964, when he had already claimed 36 wins. Tobias and his wife, Mary, founded Tobias Speed Equipment in 1961. He lost his life at 46 years of age in an accident at the USAC Sprint Car Race at Flemington Speedway. At that time, he had just won at the Indian State Fairgrounds. (Courtesy of Rick Huff Photography.)

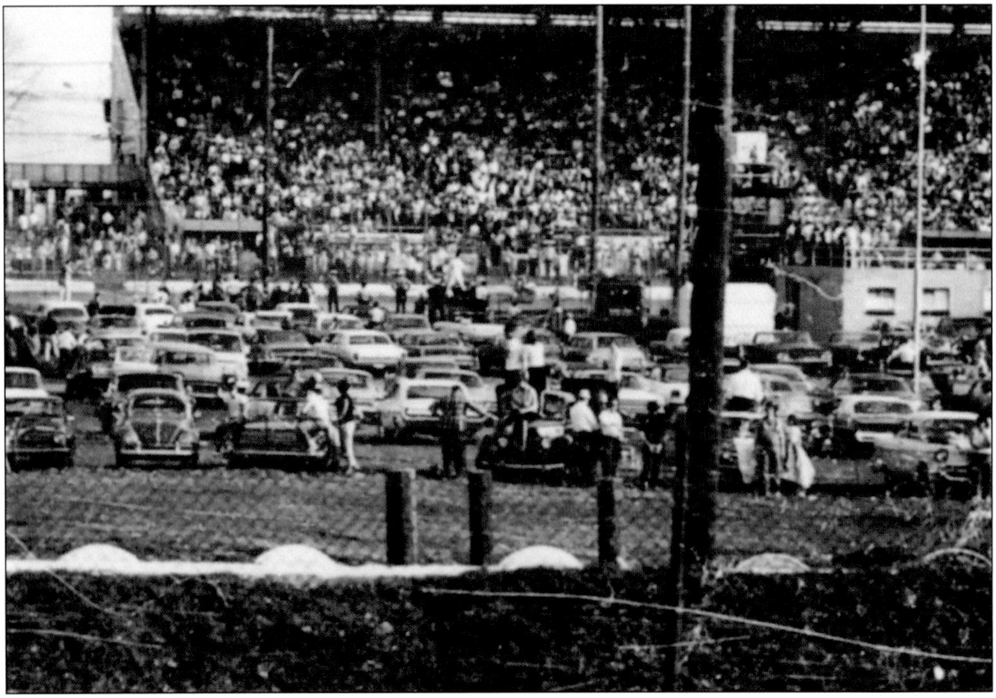

Fans, drivers, and track historians always love to reminisce about the Reading Fairgrounds Speedway since its closing in 1979. Commemorative T-shirts, mugs, and pictures have helped to keep the memories alive. The Reading Fairgrounds Racing Historical Society has continued to share knowledge of the famous track. The annual Reading Racing Reunion and Car Show is held at the Fairground Square Mall in February of each year. Tons of fans and drivers flock to the reunion to meet drivers and make new memories. The historical society has a fantastic Facebook page and an informative website that provides fans a chance to share personal pictures from their own collections and stay up to date with current events. (Both, courtesy of Fred Spiezio.)

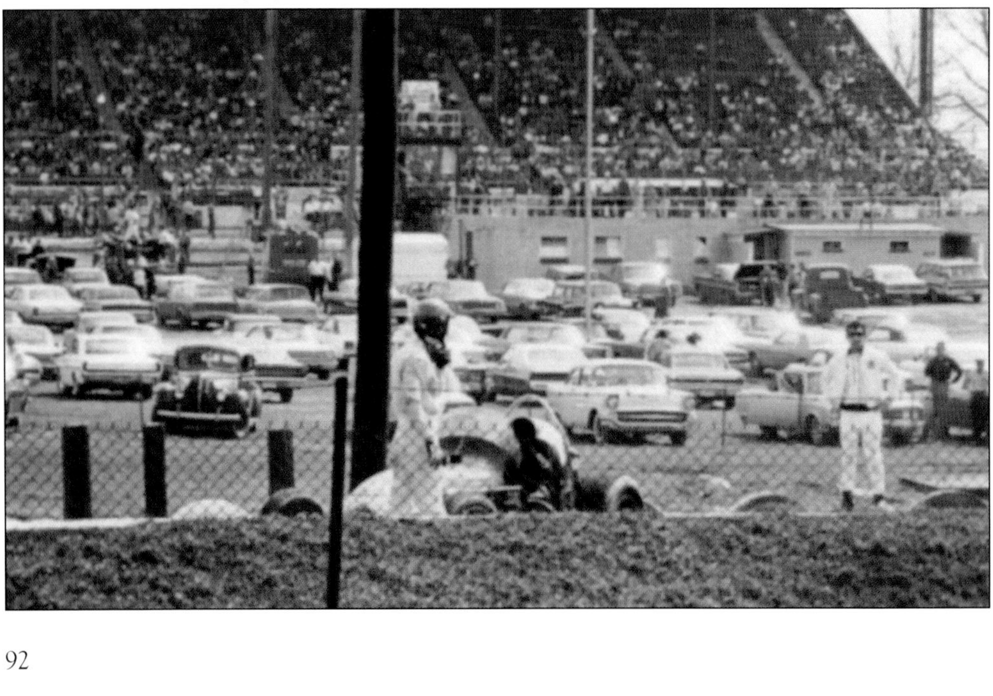

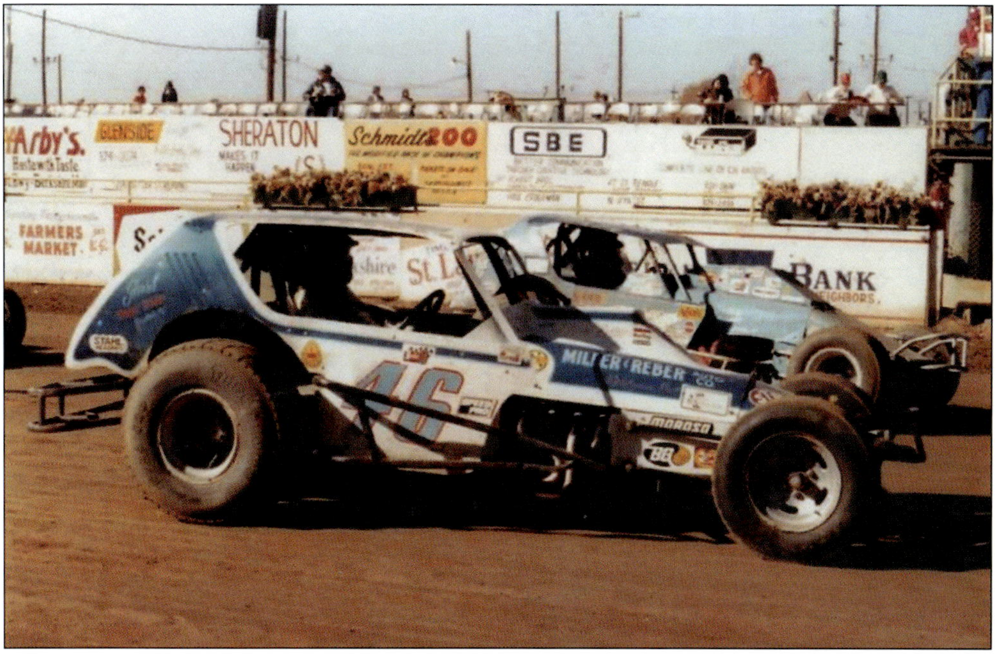

"Electrifying" Elvin Felty, of Lebanon, Pennsylvania, drove the No. 46 modified race car. He was a favorite at Reading Fairgrounds Speedway and many other tracks, such as Penn National Speedway and Silver Springs Speedway, where he was a winner. Felty still makes appearances for interviews and to meet his fans. (Courtesy of Rick Huff Photography.)

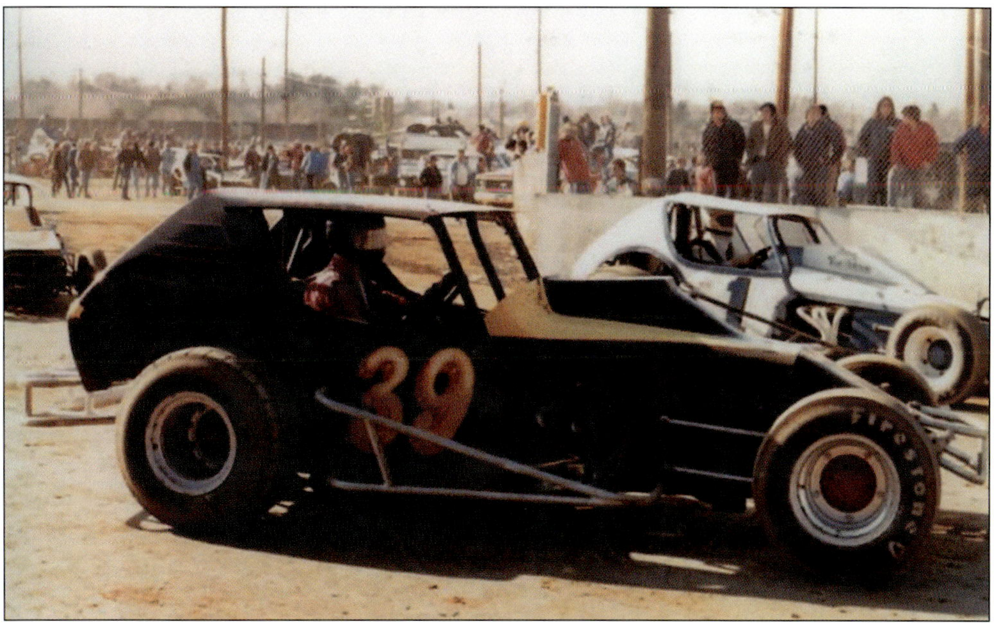

Paul Koch is shown here in the late 1970s at Reading Fairgrounds Speedway. This photograph was taken in his early years of driving. He was only 20 years old at the time and learning the ropes as a driver. He won one point champion race and had 79 wins at Grandview Speedway. Koch started quarter midget racing at age six at Hatfield Speedway and Reading Fairgrounds Speedway, where he loved the track. (Courtesy of Rick Huff Photography.)

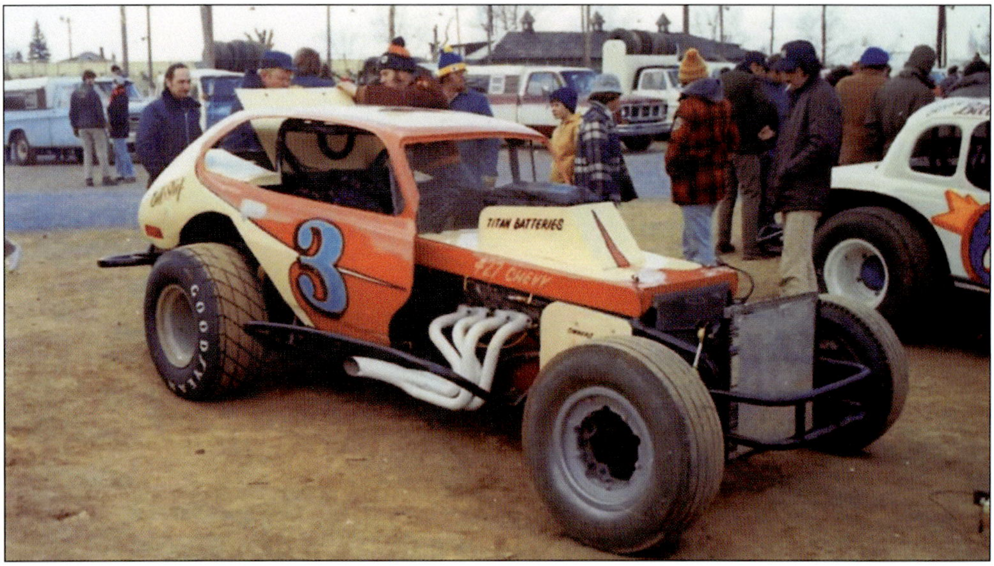

Bill Steif (No. 3) is shown here at Reading Fairgrounds Speedway in the 1970s. He raced with some other great drivers, such as Buzzie Reutiman (No. 00), Bobby Braxton (No. 10), Red Coffin (No. 26), Johnny Botz (No. 2), Earl Derr (No. 75), and Bobby Allen (No. 1 A). Many of these drivers have continued to race or work in the racing business. They continue to love the track, tell stories of great races they drove, and show the trophies they won. Reunions and banquets are great meeting places for drivers. Most dirt track drivers have had the chance to drive at other tracks in the area. Often, they would drive out of state to compete at large tracks. Fans were sometimes willing to allow the drivers to work or store their cars in their personal garages, which was very helpful. (Courtesy of Rick Huff Photography.)

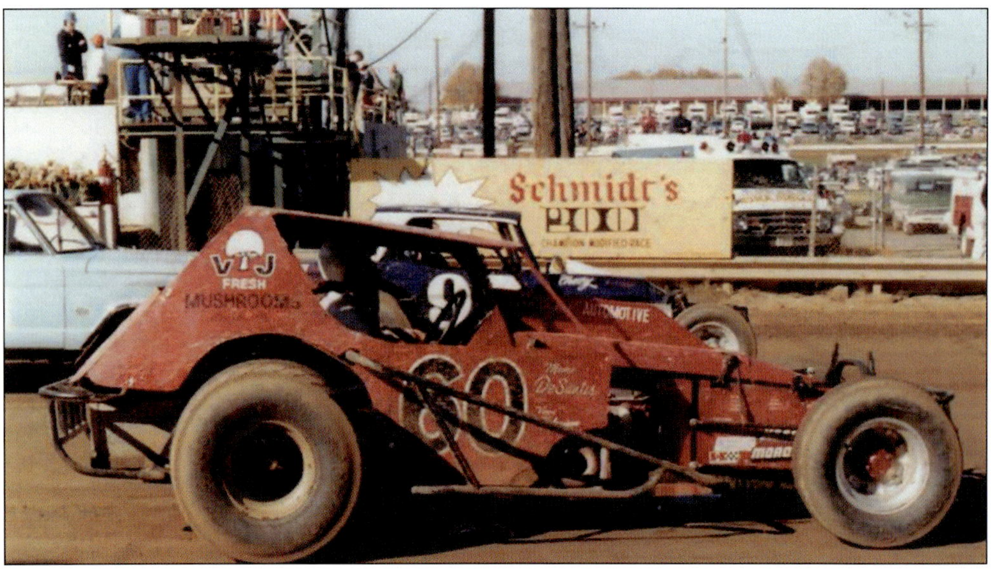

Meme Desantis, of Berks County, grew up at the track and eventually became a driver. He spent his youth admiring the great drivers of the Reading Fairgrounds Speedway, including his father, Meme Desantis Sr. He won in 1977 and continued that year with 15 top-10 finishes. In 2013, he won at Grandview Speedway. Desantis Jr. has always persevered on the track. (Courtesy of Rick Huff Photography.)

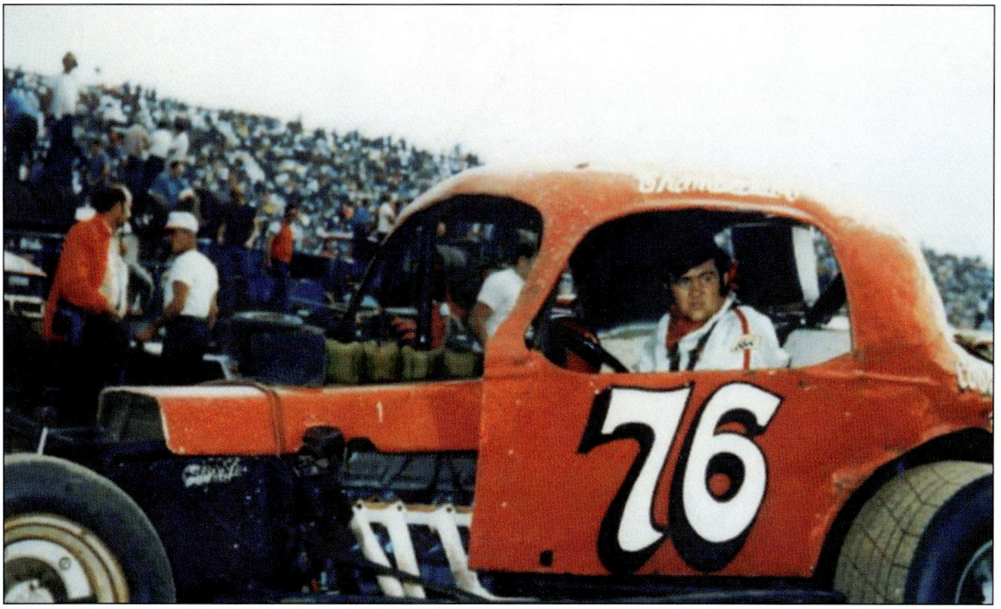

Gerald Chamberlain, known as the "Everett Express," is pictured at the Reading Fairgrounds Speedway. He won on many tracks, including two Daniel Boone 200 laps at Reading Fairgrounds in the 1970s. Chamberlain, a favorite at the track and on the Internet, has been inducted into the Dirt Motorsports Hall Of Fame. (Courtesy of Rick Huff Photography.)

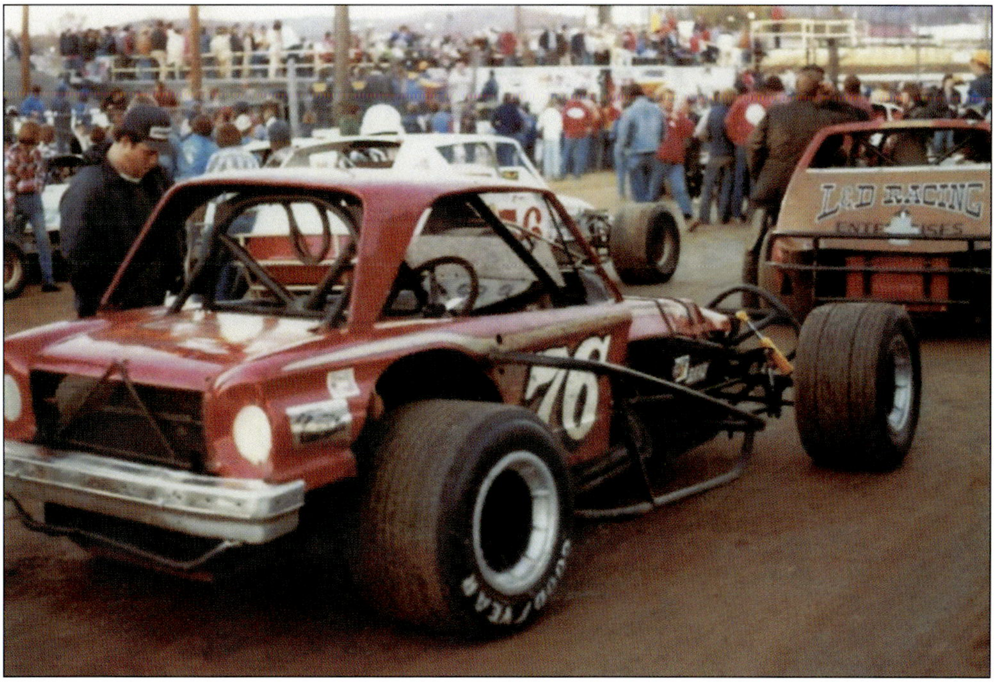